PROGRAMMING IN BASIC

The Time-Sharing Language

PRENTICE-HALL INTERNATIONAL, INC., *London*
PRENTICE-HALL OF AUSTRALIA, PTY. LTD., *Sydney*
PRENTICE-HALL OF CANADA, LTD., *Toronto*
PRENTICE-HALL OF INDIA PRIVATE LTD., *New Delhi*
PRENTICE-HALL OF JAPAN, INC., *Tokyo*

PROGRAMMING
IN BASIC
The Time-Sharing Language

Mario V. Farina

Telecommunications & Information Processing Operations
General Electric Company

PRENTICE-HALL, Inc., Englewood Cliffs, New Jersey

Current printing (last digit):
17   16   15   14   13   12

Library of Congress Catalog Card Number 68-14858
Printed in the United States of America

To

Ellinor and Don

Preface

This book is a 25-lesson introduction to the BASIC programming language as it is used on teletype time-sharing computer systems. BASIC is a language developed under the direction of Professors John G. Kemeny and Thomas E. Kurtz at Dartmouth College under the terms of a grant by the National Science Foundation.

The book is intended for:

1. Engineers who need to learn the language quickly without an instructor.

2. Computer programming students who want to practice writing computer solutions to real problems.

3. Programmers who need an easy-to-use language for checking out programs written in a more difficult programming language.

The BASIC language is used on GE-265 and GE-645 computer systems. It is ideally suited for the solution of scientific or business problems of moderate size and complexity. This text describes the language completely and provides many illustrative examples.

Many exercises are given and answers are provided for selected problems. An appendix summarizes all the BASIC commands, and a comprehensive index permits the student to find any topic quickly.

I wish to thank the many people who helped in the preparation of this text. In particular I'd like to mention William A. Hatch, and Bart R. De Rizzo, both BASIC experts.

Also, a great deal of credit must go to Mrs. B. E. Shaffer and Miss Jean Archambault for much expert typing. To Joseph L. Katz go my thanks for his suggestions and guidance.

Mario V. Farina

Contents

PROGRAMMING IN BASIC
The Time-Sharing Language

Lesson 1

DO YOU HAVE PROBLEMS?

Do you have problems?

Do those problems involve repetitive calculations using a desk calculator or a slide rule?

Why not have a computer help solve your problems?

It's easy!

All you have to do is pick up the phone and dial a computer. Here's how it works:

You sit at a teletype machine and dial the computer's telephone number. The computer responds by transmitting a high-pitched tone through the receiver. This tells you you're connected.

Now you can begin telling the computer what your problem is by typing it on the teletypewriter's keyboard. (It helps if you're a good typist but "hunt-and-peck" works almost as well.)

You present your problem in the form of statements. Each statement has a "line" number. Here's an example of a complete problem statement:

```
10 LET A = 2.4

20 LET B = 5.7

30 LET C = A * B + 15

40 PRINT C

50 END
```

Figure 1-1

In this example there are five statements; each is typed on a separate line.

Notice the line numbers. They may be any different numbers between 0 and 99999 inclusive. As you can see, you may skip numbers, but the numbers you use must be in order. The last statement must be one which reads END.

The five statements in Figure 1-1 constitute a "program." A program tells the computer what you want it to do.

You have probably already figured out what the computer is being asked to do in the program above.

First, the computer is told that A is to hold the value 2.4.

Then, the computer is told that B is to hold the value 5.7.

Next, the computer is told that it must compute A multiplied by B and add 15 to the product. The answer is assigned to C.

Finally, the computer is told to print the answer, the value of C.

In the illustration, the names used are A, B and C. Names used in programs may consist of one or two characters. If a name has only one character, the character must be a letter. If the name consists of two characters, the name must be a letter followed by a digit. Here are some legal names:

```
X
P
R
V
S3
A6
R2
V9
```

Figure 1-2

These names are not legal:

ALPHA   (too long)

6X   (names cannot begin with a digit)

8   (one-character names cannot be a digit)

PQ   (two-character names must consist of a
                         letter and a digit)

Figure 1-3

EXERCISE (for practice)

What's wrong with this program?

```
10  LET XY = -25

15  LET 6P = 16.2

25  J = XY + 6P + D

20  PRIND J
```

Figure 1-4

Answers:

1. XY is not a legal name.

2. 6P is not a legal name.

3. Line 20 is out of order. The number should be 26 or greater.

4. PRINT is spelled wrong.

5. D cannot be used in the calculation. It hasn't been given a value.

6. The word LET is missing in statement 25.

7. The statement reading END is missing.

EXERCISE (now you try it)

What's wrong with this program:

Lesson 1

```
15 W6 = -6.5

20 LET PI = 3.1416

30 LET C = 2 * PI * W6

30 PRINT C

   LET F = 29.6

35 LET E = D + D

40 PRINT E

50 FINIS
```

Figure 1-5

Errors:

1.

2.

3.

4.

5.

6.

Lesson 2

WHAT IS BASIC?

In Lesson 1 we gave a very simple illustration of how to write a program. You saw the use of such words as LET, PRINT and END.

The words are part of a language which has been devised for telling a computer what to do. That language is called BASIC. It is one of the languages used when communicating with a computer.

There are other BASIC words you can use. Some of them are:

> READ
> GØ
> IF
> FØR
> DATA
> NEXT
> TØ
> INPUT

There are a few more which we'll introduce as we go along.

BASIC is a problem-solving language. It is ideally suited for use where equations must be evaluated.

In writing equations you may use these arithmetic symbols:

> +   (add)
> -   (subtract)
> *   (multiply)
> /   (divide)
> ↑   (raise to a power)

Lesson 2

Let's see how some equations would be written:

equation: p = r x s + t

BASIC: 15 LET P = R* S + T

The line number can be any number you choose.

equation: $b = \dfrac{c + d}{e} - 6$

BASIC: 325 LET B = (C + D)/E - 6

Note the use of parentheses to make the meaning of the equation clear.

equation: $\alpha = \lambda + \Delta + 29$

BASIC: 99 LET A = L + D + 29

Greek letters cannot be typed. You must invent names for α, λ and Δ.

equation: $k = m^5 - n^{10.6}$

BASIC: 22 LET K = M ↑ 5 - N ↑ 10.6

Lesson 2

If you have access to a teletype machine connected to a computer, you should begin writing programs at once. Practice with the ones shown in this book. Make up new ones as soon as you're able.

When you write a statement, type the line number, then write the statement on the same line. <u>Spacing</u> <u>is</u> <u>not</u> <u>important.</u> Put plenty of spaces between your symbols or none at all; it's all the same to the computer. However, for neatness sake, put spaces in as you would if you were writing a letter to a friend.

At the end of each line, <u>hit the RETURN key.</u> If you make a mistake, retype the entire statement. (We'll show you a better way to make corrections later.)

EXERCISE

What's wrong with these independent BASIC equations:

15 LET C = (D + E) K

20 W = P + R6

25 LET N = Y * Y * Y * Y * Y * Y

30 LET F = G / * H

35 LET B4 = W + C7) / E9

Lesson 3

WHAT IS TELETYPE TIME SHARING?

Imagine a GE computer at some central location, say downtown New York, operated by an organization which offers a computing service. One may avail himself of this service by sitting at a teletype machine, picking up a telephone attached to the machine, and dialing the computer.

The computer users are all at remote points from one another. However, since they have subscribed to the service, they are permitted to "call up" the computer at any time. (The service is usually available at least 16 hours a day, 6 days a week.) The subscribers get a bill once a month for the computing service they've had during the previous month.

Many subscribers can be connected to the same computer at one time, yet it appears to each person as if he's the only one actually using the computer at any one moment. The reason this illusion is possible is because the computer's time is "shared." While one user is typing a message on the teletypewriter, no actual computer time is being used by that person. The computer can, therefore, be doing calculations for someone else.

Similarly, while answers are coming back (being typed out) to the user, actual computer time is not being used. Calculating can be in progress for another subscriber.

While still another subscriber is "thinking" while sitting at his teletype machine, or leafing through handbooks, or indulging in casual conversation with a visitor, the computer can be, and usually is, computing for someone else.

A computer is fast; it can execute hundreds of thousands of instructions per second. It, therefore, has very little difficulty serving 40, 50, or even more subscribers. Very rarely will a person have to wait when he's ready to compute, and then only for a few seconds. It is, therefore, perfectly feasible for many subscribers to "share time" on a distant computer.

Let's say that Joe Brown is an engineer who wants to solve a mathematical problem quickly. He turns to his teletype machine, presses a button marked ORIG and dials the computer's phone number.

The computer types a message to the user saying, in effect, ''I am here waiting to serve you.'' Then the computer types out:

USER NUMBER --

The subscriber types his user number* and returns the teletypewriter's carriage. Here's what the user's reply may look like. (The example user number is fictitious):

USER NUMBER -- X99999

The computer will then want to know what computer language Joe intends to use. Three languages are available: FORTRAN, ALGOL and BASIC.

The BASIC language is, by far, the easiest to use of the three. It is the one we'll describe in this book.

The computer's message and Joe Brown's answer look like this:

SYSTEM --- BASIC

Now the computer will want to know whether Joe intends to write a new program or use one he wrote and saved another day. Assume he intends to write a new one. The computer will type and Joe will reply:

NEW ØR ØLD -- NEW

---

*On Model 35 teletypes, the user will have to push a <u>button</u> marked ''K'' before the computer will accept his number. Careful, this is not the key K but a button located to the left of the keyboard.

The computer will now request a name for the new program. That name may have up to 6 characters:

NEW PRØBLEM NAME -- EQS

Finally, the computer types:

READY

Now the computer user may begin typing his problem into the computer. If he makes a mistake along the way, the computer will politely tell him and give him a chance to correct it.

Finally, when the entire program has been entered, the user types:

RUN

and the computer will solve the problem. Answers will be typed by the computer immediately following the word RUN.

After Joe has received his answers, he may want to save the program so that he can use it again another day. In order to do this, he types:

SAVE

The computer will save the program at the computer site.

Joe signs off by typing:

GØØDBYE

or

BYE

Lesson 3

Suppose Joe Brown is faced with the necessity to solve the same problem the next day. Joe can turn again to his teletype machine, dial up the computer and converse with it as follows:

```
USER NUMBER -- X99999
SYSTEM -- BASIC
NEW ØR ØLD -- ØLD
ØLD PRØBLEM NAME -- EQS
READY.
```

The computer types the word READY indicating that it has retrieved the user's program, and has made it available to him. If the user wants to, he can now change parts of the program; then run it.

When he's done, he can simply type:

```
BYE
```

It is not necessary to type SAVE again. However, if he wants to "unsave" his program, he can type:

```
UNSAVE
```

before he signs off.

Briefly, this is how time sharing and the BASIC programming language can be used by engineers, statisticians, market forecasters and others who want fast answers to relatively simple problems.

We haven't answered all your questions; you must have hundreds of them. But read through this little book, work out the exercises, and try programs of your own. Toward the end of the book there are several "system" commands you can try. For now you don't need to know them.

Here is the keyboard you'll be working with. It's for a Model 33 Teletype Unit, which is the one most in use. It's possible that your machine is a Model 35. If so, some of the keys and buttons we mention in this book will be different. In general, this will not inconvenience you, but if you do have some problems, we suggest you call your sales representative for assistance.

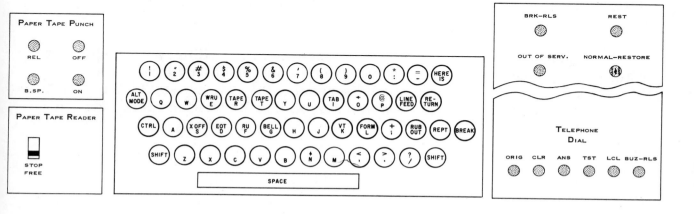

Figure 3-1

EXERCISE

Without looking back at the text unless you have to, write down what the distant computer types out to you and what you reply when you want to give it a new problem to solve. Assume you've dialed, the computer has "beeped," and you've pushed the ORIG button.

Lesson 4

FLOWCHARTING, THE LANGUAGE OF LOGIC

A computer, by itself, can do nothing. It has to be told what to do completely and precisely. A person, wanting to use a computer, must plan ahead of time exactly what he wants the computer to do.

Such planning can, of course, be written down in ordinary English. For example, suppose it is desired to have the computer calculate 2^{15} and have the computer print out 15 intermediate results (2^1, 2^2, 2^3, etc.). We could write down a plan for having the computer do this by writing these English statements:

STEPS	What the computer must do
1.	Set power equal to 1.
2.	Raise 2 by the power.
3.	Print out the answer.
4.	Does the power equal 15. If so, stop computer. If not, add 1 to the power.
5.	Repeat this procedure beginning with step 2 above.

This sort of planning is OK, but it requires a lot of writing. Its meaning is difficult to grasp at a glance. It's a cumbersome method to use where complicated procedures are involved.

A pictorial method for showing a problem solution is used by people who work with computers. That method is called "flow charting."

A computer user shows what he wants the computer to do by drawing a chart. That chart consists of rectangles, diamonds, circles and other shapes. Inside the shapes are written what the computer is to do. The computer user shows what is to happen first, what next, etc., by joining the shapes with arrows. The completed chart is called a "flow chart."

Here is a flow chart showing the pictorial planning for the problem described above:

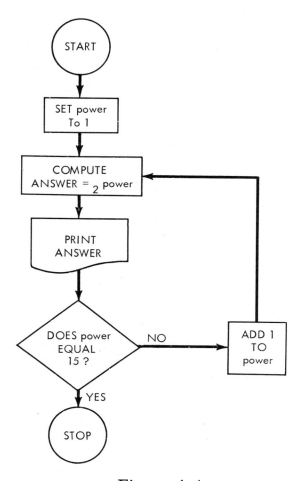

Figure 4-1

The flow chart shows a "loop." A loop is a series of operations which are repeated over and over. Here, the equation ANSWER = 2^{power} is evaluated 15 times.

You're probably wondering about the meanings of the shapes used in the flow chart. We'll explain them shortly. First, though, let's see what the BASIC program corresponding to the flow chart looks like:

```
10 LET P = 1

20 LET A = 2 ↑ P

25 PRINT A

35 IF P = 15 THEN 90

45 LET P = P + 1

50 GØ TØ 20

90 STØP

99999 END
```

Figure 4-2

There are a number of points to be observed here. First, at line number 10 you can see how a variable name is given some value. A name is typed, and following it, an "equals" sign is written. To the right of the "equals" sign is the value assigned to the name.

The statement at line 45 may be puzzling:

```
45 P = P + 1
```

Certainly in mathematics P cannot equal P + 1. It doesn't in BASIC either. The statement has an entirely different meaning. It means "make the calculation indicated at the right of the 'equals' sign and assign the result of the calculation to the name shown at the left of the 'equals' sign."

The old value of P is used when making the calculation. The value 1 is added to it, and the result becomes the "updated" value of P. The old value of P is replaced. It is completely lost. But that's all right, isn't it? After all, the old value of P is no longer needed. These last two paragraphs are very important. Please read them again.

At line number 50, we have a ''branch'' statement:

50 GØ TØ 20

This kind of branch is called an ''unconditional'' branch, because the computer is unconditionally instructed to go back to line number 20.

At line number 35, there is a ''conditional'' branch. The computer is instructed to jump to line number 90 if, and only if, P equals 15. Here is that statement:

35 IF P = 15 THEN 90

If P does not equal 15, the computer will not branch to line number 90. It will go to the <u>next</u> statement in the program instead. In this case, the next statement is located at line number 45.

Line number 99999 is used to hold the END statement. We recommend you use this line number for all your END statements because it is the highest line number possible in BASIC. Since END must be the last statement of any BASIC program, you can't go wrong by automatically inserting:

99999 END

in all your programs.

Notice the slight difference between a flow chart and the BASIC coding which corresponds to the flow chart. The chart uses the names ''power'' and ''ANSWER.'' Since these words are illegal as BASIC names, you can choose names which are as close as possible to those words; hence the names P and A.

Of course, any names you choose would be OK, but names chosen should remind you what they stand for.

A flow chart once written is easily transformed into BASIC statements. The major effort in writing a BASIC program lies in the development of the flow chart. The <u>procedure</u> that the computer is to use is shown on the chart.

Let's nail down a few important concepts now:

1. A computer does not solve problems. The computer user does. He shows the procedure that the computer is to follow by drawing a flow chart. Then he writes BASIC statements in accordance with the flow chart.

2. The process of developing a procedure that the computer is to use is called "programming."

3. The typed BASIC statements which exist when a computer user has transformed a flow chart to computer instructions, is called a "program."

All computer programming should include the writing of a flow chart unless the problem being solved is extremely simple. Taking short cuts in this area can get you into a peck of trouble.

A flow chart doesn't spring up full grown from the start. There is much "cutting and trying" required. The computer user thinks with a pencil in his hand. He jots down an idea, changes it, erases it, revamps it. Gradually, as his thinking crystallizes, the chart takes final form. At this point, the difficult part is over. The BASIC statements almost write themselves.

What is needed during flow-chart development is an active mind, lots of paper, a sharp pencil, and a large eraser.

Despite the fact that flow charting is so important in computer programming, there is surprisingly little conformity regarding how different people chart the same problem. Flow charts can be compared to works of art. The shapes vary, their placements on paper are often arbitrary, but well-drawn flow charts are easily understood by computer users in much the same way that a Yankee understands a Southern drawl.

Lesson 4

Here are some shapes that are widely used by professional problem-solvers. Their meanings are also shown:

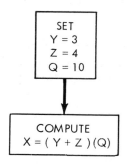

Figure 4-3

Rectangles show calculations to be made or initial values to be assigned.

These boxes would be rendered in BASIC as:

50 LET Y = 3

60 LET Z = 4

70 LET Q = 10

80 LET X = (Y + Z) * Q

Figure 4-4

Note the slight difference between the way the statement is written at line 50, and the equation's representation in the corresponding rectangles of the flow chart. You may take all the liberties you like in the flow chart so long as the BASIC statements are written correctly.

Figure 4-5

This shape is used to indicate that the computer is to print out a message. Here's an example of how this shape is transformed into a BASIC statement:

225 PRINT "THIS PRØGRAM CØMPUTES 5 RHØ CALCS"

You can probably guess what will happen when the statement at line number 225 is executed. We'll cover details of the PRINT statement in an early lesson. Don't be concerned if you don't fully understand it now.

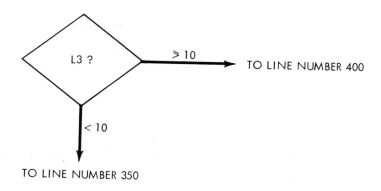

Figure 4-6

A diamond shape indicates that the computer is to make a decision. We'll see what kinds of decisions the computer can make, when we discuss the IF statement. For now, we'll simply show one BASIC statement which agrees with the above diamond:

300 IF L3 > = 10 THEN 400

350 LET J = 0

400 LET K = 0

Figure 4-7

If L3 is equal to, or greater than 10, the computer jumps to line number 400; if L3 is less than 10, the computer goes to the next statement in sequence. In this case, if L3 is less than 10, the computer goes to line number 350, and continues the program from that point. Statement 400 can be several statements removed from line number 300 where the IF statement is shown.

Lesson 4

Figure 4-8

Circles or oval shapes are used to show the beginning or stopping points of programs. Note their uses here:

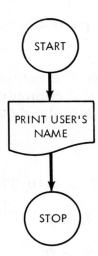

Figure 4-9

Here is the corresponding BASIC program:

50 PRINT ''MY NAME IS JØE BRØWN''

60 STØP

99999 END

Figure 4-10

This is a complete BASIC program. There is no BASIC statement equivalent to the ''start'' shape in the flow chart. None is necessary.

Here's a simple practice exercise. Draw the flow chart which corresponds to the following BASIC program:

10 LET X = 0

110 LET X = X + 1

120 GØ TØ 110

99999 END

Figure 4-11

This is an easy one and looks like this:

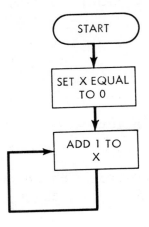

Figure 4-12

You can see this is a foolish little program. The value of X is increased by 1 in a "tight" loop. The program could run forever; there's no provision to stop the computer.

Don't worry about this. In actual practice you can stop a program like this by typing the letter S on the teletypewriter's keyboard. This can be done even while the computer is typing.

A word of warning: typing the letter S while the computer is typing will sometimes disconnect you from the computer. Form the habit from the beginning of holding down the CONTROL and SHIFT KEYS simultaneously and hitting the letter P at the same time. This is a much safer way of stopping a program before it comes to its normal termination point. The CONTROL key is the one marked CTRL at the left of the keyboard.

Lesson 4

Here's another practice exercise. Transform this flow chart to a
BASIC program:

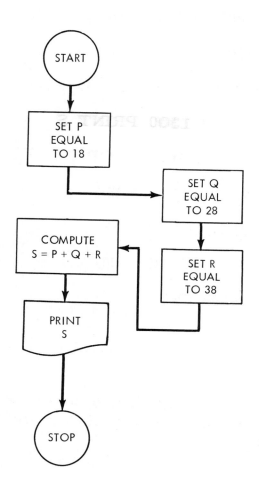

Figure 4-13

One way to write the program is this:

```
1000 LET P = 18

1100 GØ TØ 2000

1200 LET S = P + Q + R

1300 PRINT S

1400 STØP

2000 LET Q = 28

2100 LET R = 38

2200 GØ TØ 1200

99999 END
```

Figure 4-14

Again, this is a rather foolish way to write the program, but it follows the flow chart closely. You can see that this next BASIC program accomplishes the same purpose:

```
1000 LET P = 18

1100 LET Q = 28

1200 LET R = 38

1300 LET S = P + Q + R

1400 PRINT S

1500 STØP

99999 END
```

Figure 4-15

When the STOP statement is the last statement of a program preceding the END statement, it can be omitted. In this illustration, line number 1500 need not exist. In Figure 4-14, line number 1400 is essential. Can you see why? What would happen if it wasn't there?

EXERCISE

Have the computer set B equal to zero and D equal to zero. Then have the computer multiply B by D and print out the answer. Next, have the computer increase B by 1 and D by 1, and have it repeat the multiplication and print-out. Keep increasing B and D by 1, and repeating the procedure described until the answer exceeds 25000. At that point have the computer

Write the flow chart first; then write the BASIC program which solves the problem.

Lesson 5

TELLING THE COMPUTER ABOUT NUMBERS

A great many computer-type problems involve three simple steps:

1. Telling the computer what numbers are needed in your program.
2. Telling the computer what to do with those numbers.
3. Having the computer print out answers.

This lesson will be concerned with how to tell the computer what numbers are needed in your program.

One easy way to tell the computer about numbers used in your program is to give each of those numbers a name. Here's how it's done:

$$500 \text{ LET } A = 2.4$$

$$600 \text{ LET } B = -6.7$$

$$700 \text{ LET } C = A + B$$

800 PRINT C

$$900 \text{ LET } B = -1.2$$

$$1000 \text{ LET } C = A - B$$

1100 PRINT C

99999 END

Figure 5-1

Lesson 5

This is a complete BASIC program. A is set to 2.4 at line number 500. B is set to -6.7 at line number 600. Notice that B is changed at line number 900. The old value of B, -6.7, is lost at that time. The new value of B, -1.2, replaces the old value.

Note that the value for A remains constant in this program at 2.4. This is because nothing happens in the program to change it.

What about C? Does its value change in the program? The answer is yes. At line number 700, C is set to A plus B. The computer calculates the sum of A and B (algebraically) and finds that the answer is -4.3 (2.4 plus (-6.7) = -4.3). That value is assigned to C.

At line number 1000, C is calculated again. This time the result is found to be 3.6.(2.4 minus (-1.2) = 3.6). You can see that the value for A is 2.4 (nothing has happened to change it), but the value for B is -1.2 (B was changed at line number 900).

Now study this instructive little program:

```
10 LET I = 1

20 LET P = 1

30 LET N = I + P

40 PRINT N

50 IF P = 40 THEN 99999

60 LET I = I + 1

70 LET P = P + 1

80 GØ TØ 30

99999 END
```

Figure 5-2

The values of I and P keep changing repeatedly in this program. If you study the program you'll see that 40 calculations are made. At line number 50 the value of P is tested. If it equals 40, the program stops. If it does not, the computer adds 1 to I and to P; then repeats the calculation N = I + P.

Since I and P always have the same value, the test to determine whether the computer should stop can be made with I as well as with P.

To summarize, you can invent a name and assign to that name a numeric value, either positive or negative. That value will remain constant unless deliberately changed by the program.

Another way to tell the computer about numbers is to include those numbers in a DATA statement. Here's how that's done:

```
5 READ A1

10 READ A2

15 LET F = A1 * A2

20 PRINT F

25 GØ TØ 5

30 DATA 6, 7.2, -3.1, 1.2, 4.8, 9

99999 END
```

Figure 5-3

You'll notice two new kinds of statements in this program. The DATA statement at line number 30 shows a list of six numbers separated by commas. There are READ statements at line numbers 5 and 10.

The way the program works is this:

Lesson 5

Execution of the READ statement at line number 5 causes one of the values in the DATA statement to be used. It is assigned the name A1. That value is 6. Similarly, execution of the READ statement at line number 10 causes another value in the DATA statement to be used. The next value in the DATA statement, 7.2, is assigned the name A2.

The calculation indicated at line number 15 is performed. That is, A1 is multiplied by A2, and the result is assigned the name F.

Observe the unconditional branch at line number 25. The computer is instructed to return to the statement at line number 5. The statements at line numbers 5 and 10 will cause two more values to be "read" from the DATA statement. These two will be the next two unused values. They are -3.1 and 1.2. Those values will be assigned to A1 and A2 respectively.

Again the calculation giving F is made, and again an unconditional branch is made to the beginning of the program.

A third set of two values is taken from the DATA statement. A third calculation is made, and another branch is made to line 5. At this point the computer will stop. It won't find any more values to use in the DATA statement. The next "read" will be unsuccessful because there are no more values in the DATA statement, and this will cause the program to be terminated.

Here are a few important points to be aware of:

1. The READ statement can "read" more than one value from the DATA statement at a time. Example: READ X, Y, Z.

2. DATA statements may appear anywhere in a BASIC program.

3. There may be any number of DATA statements sprinkled in a program. They are accessed in the same order that they appear in the program.

4. Values in DATA statements are separated by commas.

Let's look at this next program which computes the circumferences of several circles. The values given in the DATA statements are radii:

```
10 DATA 2.6, 1.2, 9.7

20 READ R

25 LET C = 2 * 3.1416 * R

30 DATA 9.5, 10.6

40 PRINT C

50 GØ TØ 20

55 DATA 9.1, 14.5, 8, 4.5

99999 END
```

Figure 5-4

The computer reads successive values of R, computes C, prints out C, then goes back to line number 20 to process another case. The fact that the DATA statements are interspersed in the program is immaterial. It's not very neat but it's all right.

The values assigned to R are 2.6, 1.2, 9.7, 9.5, 10.6, 9.1, 14.5, 8 and 4.5, in that order.

We recommend that when you write DATA statements, you place them all together, either at the beginning or near the end of your program.

Note how this program is written:

Lesson 5

```
10 READ A, B, C

20 LET D = A + B + C

30 PRINT D

40 GØ TØ 10

50 DATA 5, 6, 7, 4, -2, -4, 8, 4, 7, 82

60 DATA 90, 92, -1, -3, 5

99999 END
```

Figure 5-5

At line number 10, the READ statement shows that each set of values read will contain three numbers. A set of numbers is not limited to 3. Four, five, or more numbers can be read in with one READ statement.

A glance at the two DATA statements will show that there are 5 sets of 3 values each. Observe that values in a DATA statement must be separated by commas, and that part of a set can be in one DATA statement and the other part in another DATA statement. The values 82, 90 and 92 are members of one set but they are recorded in two DATA statements. There is no comma following 82.

The use of DATA statements is a very convenient way to tell the computer about which numbers to use. Many numbers can be given to the computer quickly and compactly. Furthermore, if this program is saved at the computer site and brought back into use another day, the only statements to change before the program is run again, are the DATA statements.

We'll give details about how to save and change programs when we introduce "System Features."

We said earlier that when the computer runs out of data, it stops. This is true, but this may not always be what you want. One way to avoid having the computer stop after reading an entire list of data items is to put a "dummy" value at the end of the list for which the computer can check. Study this example:

```
100  READ X

110  IF X = 999 THEN 150

120  LET Y = X ↑ 3

130  PRINT Y, X

140  GØ TØ 100

150  PRINT "END ØF PRØGRAM"

160  DATA 2, 18, 91, 42, -6, 14, -62, 999

99999  END
```

Figure 5-6

When a value of X is read, it is checked against value 999. That value is a "dummy." That is, it is a value which the computer user is certain will never be an actual value to process. When it is found, the computer is directed to branch to the statement at line number 150. There the message "END OF PROGRAM" is printed and the computer stops.

Of course much more can be done beginning with the statement at line number 150 than just print out the simple message shown.

The program shows that whenever the value of X, which is read, is some value other than 999, it is used in subsequent statements.

The IF statement is a very powerful one. We'll be describing it completely in a lesson soon.

In this lesson you've seen that there are two ways to tell the computer about numbers. One way is to "build" those numbers into the program by assigning a name to each one. Example:

*30 LET J3 = -6.45

The other way is to show numbers in DATA statements and have the computer "read" them. Example:

50 READ X, Y, Z
60 DATA 2.45, 6.78, 9.42, 7.65, 8.42, -7.64

EXERCISE

Write a BASIC program which calculates the area of at least 10 circles. Use READ and DATA statements in your program. Recall that Area = πr^2. For π use the value 3.1416.

* See Lesson 24 for additional LET features.

Lesson 6

EXPONENTIAL NOTATION

In this short lesson we'll introduce an alternate way of writing numbers in your program. That method is called exponential notation. A number is expressed as some value times some power of 10.

For example:

$$1.654E4 \text{ means } 1.654 \times 10^4 \text{ or } 16540.$$

The letter E in the number, then, can be read as "times 10 to the -- power."

Powers can be positive or negative. Thus, 3E-2 means 3×10^{-2}. Since 10^{-2} means .01, the number being expressed is .03.

Here are some powers of 10 to show the pattern:

$$
\begin{aligned}
10^3 &\text{ means } 1000 \\
10^2 &\text{ means } 100 \\
10^1 &\text{ means } 10 \\
10^0 &\text{ means } 1 \\
10^{-1} &\text{ means } .1 \\
10^{-2} &\text{ means } .01 \\
10^{-3} &\text{ means } .001
\end{aligned}
$$

Numbers in exponential notation can be used in BASIC statements wherever ordinary decimal numbers are needed. Here are some examples:

```
10 LET B = -1.5E-3

20 LET C = 2.456E12

30 READ D

40 LET E = B * C * D * 3E3

50 PRINT E

60 GØ TØ 30

70 DATA 1.6E2, 9.4E3, 16, 9.4E-2, 146.7

99999 END
```

Figure 6-1

The example shows that numbers in both ordinary decimal notation and in exponential notation can be used in the same program.

When writing a number in exponential notation, a maximum of 9 significant digits can be used. These numbers are OK:

45.2341239E6
-1.45236745E-1
492345673E27

Maximum values that numbers can reach when expressed in exponential notation are in the order of $1 \times 10^{\pm 38}$. If the computer being used permits it, numbers as large as $1 \times 10^{\pm 76}$ are possible.

EXERCISES

1. What's wrong with these BASIC statements:

           30 LET F = 1.4E*3
           40 LET G = E35
           50 LET H = 1.732415623E-2

2. Write these numbers in exponential notation:

                    -14.6
                     .00034
                    21.146

Lesson 7

TELLING THE COMPUTER WHAT TO DO WITH NUMBERS

As we've seen before, there are three simple steps involved when dealing with the solution of computer-type problems.

1. Telling the computer what numbers are used in the program.

2. Telling the computer what to do with those numbers.

3. Having the computer print out answers.

In the last two lessons you saw how one tells the computer what numbers are used in a program. In this lesson, we'll describe how you can tell the computer what to do with those numbers. Where BASIC is concerned, this means, mainly, telling the computer how to do arithmetic.

When doing arithmetic, the symbols + - * / and ↑ are used. These mean add, subtract, multiply, divide and "raise to a power."

Suppose we have this equation to write:

$$y = \frac{b + c}{d - e} + 6$$

In BASIC, it would be written like this:

$$200 \text{ LET } Y = (B + C) / (D - E) + 6$$

Of course the line number you use, can be any convenient number you select.

The equation has to be written <u>all</u> <u>on</u> <u>one</u> <u>line</u>. This is no special problem most of the time, but when divides are involved, parentheses may be necessary. The reason for using parentheses is to make sure the computer knows exactly what you want it to do, that the statement is unambiguous.

For instance suppose the equation is this:

$$a = \frac{b}{c + d}$$

You wouldn't write the BASIC statement like this:

20 LET A = B/C + D

This makes it look as if the equation really was:

$$a = \frac{b}{c} + d$$

which, of course, isn't right.

Use parentheses, and the meaning of the statement will be crystal clear:

20 LET A = B/ (C + D)

If you ever have any doubts whether or not a pair of parentheses are necessary, put them in. They won't hurt your program in any way; they won't make it run slower or be less efficient. Leave out necessary parentheses, on the other hand, and you're in trouble.

Parentheses may be written within parentheses. For example, suppose we have this equation to write:

Lesson 7

$$h = \frac{\dfrac{p + q}{r + s}}{t + v} \cdot (x + y)$$

You could write it like this:

50 LET H = ((P + Q) / ((R + S) / (T + V))) * (X + Y)

The only difficulty here is that there is only one kind of right and left parentheses permissible in BASIC. They are (and). Be careful when you use parentheses, making sure that there is a (for every) you use and vice versa

When writing a BASIC equation, only one name may be shown on the left-hand side of the equals sign. This is because of the meaning that a BASIC equation has. The calculation indicated at the right-hand side of the equation is made and the one answer which results must be assigned to the one name appearing at the left-hand side of the equals sign.

For instance, consider this example:

150 LET P = R ↑ 2 + X * T + 7

First R is squared and the result is added to the product of X times T; finally the value 7 is added. The result of the computation is assigned to the name P.

You can see that the BASIC statement:

205 K = K + 1

is perfectly legal. To the old value of K is added 1, and the result is as-signed the name K. This assignment destroys the old value of K as the new value of K is calculated.

In BASIC, statements such as the one shown above are often used where simple counting is necessary; for example, counting the number of iterations through a loop.

Whenever the computer executes a statement written in BASIC, all of the names shown on the right-hand side of the equals sign <u>must</u> <u>have</u> <u>been</u> <u>given</u> <u>values</u> <u>earlier</u> <u>in</u> <u>the</u> <u>program</u>.

Look at this program:

```
10 LET C = F + G

20 LET F = 7

30 LET G = 8

40 PRINT C

99999 END
```

Figure 7-1

The value of C when it is printed will be 0 (zero). You can see why: F and G have no values at the time the statement at line number 10 is executed.

If you correct this program by writing:

```
10 LET F = 7

20 LET G = 8

30 LET C = F + G

40 PRINT C

99999 END
```

Figure 7-2

the correct value of C, 15, will be printed when the statement at line number 40 is executed.

The upwards printing arrow means "raise to a power" (exponentiate). Therefore:

20 LET B = C ↑ 5

means "let B = C^5."

Another way to write the same statement is this way:

28 LET B = C * C * C * C * C

The latter method can be a tedius way of raising some value to a power. Try writing $g = h^{30}$ the hard way. You won't like it.

A power can be a name. This statement is OK:

30 LET K = L ↑ Q

The value of L is raised to the Q power. Of course when the statement is executed, Q must have some value. Suppose Q has the value 10; L is raised to the 10th power.

Powers don't have to be integers (whole numbers). They can be numbers like 2.7 or 1.3. Powers can also be negative. Equations such as this one are perfectly all right:

75 LET R = (V ↑ 3.2) * (Y ↑ - 1.5)

The mathematical equivalent of this BASIC statement is:

$$r = v^{3.2} \cdot y^{-1.5}$$

The last illustration shows that a multiplication symbol cannot be left out when multiplication is to be alone. Observe:

$$c = (d + e) (f + 7)$$

In BASIC this is written:

$$25 \text{ LET } C = (D + E) * (F + 7)$$

Unless parentheses in an equation direct the computer otherwise, the computer performs exponentiation operations first; multiplications and/or divisions next; and additions and/or subtractions last.

Be careful about insidious traps. Look at this statement:

$$40 \text{ LET } P = -B \uparrow 3$$

The mathematical equivalent to this statement is

$$p = -(b^3)$$

If you need $(-b)^3$, your statement must read:

$$40 \text{ LET } P = (-B) \uparrow 3$$

EXERCISES

Tell what's wrong with these independent BASIC statements:

```
 10 LET (A + B = C ↑ 3 + M
 20 N = (P + 6) * (Q + R)
 30 LET V = ((W + Z) / (A + B)
 40 LET B = D * / E + 17
 50 LET (F1 + F2) / F3 = G
 60 LET T = (I ÷ J) * (D - E)
 70 LET (W + Y) / 2
 80 LET N = P = (Q + R) * W
 90 LET M = (N * N1) (S + L)
100 LET Z = R ** T
```

Lesson 8

BUILT-IN FUNCTIONS

Equations may involve sines, cosines, logs, square roots, and other functions. These equations are easily written in BASIC. Here's an example:

$$q = \sqrt{r + s}$$

In BASIC, the statement looks like this:

50 LET Q = SQR (R + S)

Note how easily the square root of r + s is obtained. Simply call for the built-in function SQR, and place within parentheses the expression which the computer is to work with. When the equation is executed, the computer will calculate the square root of R + S, and assign the result to the name Q.

You can have the computer take the square root of a single value or of a complicated expression. Here are some legal ways that SQR can be used:

20 LET S = SQR (146.7)
30 LET T = SQR (V)
40 LET W = SQR ((A + B) / C)
50 LET C = SQR (D ↑ 3 + SQR (J))

Regardless of how SQR is used, the information which the computer is to work with, is shown within parentheses. You'll see that within parentheses can be shown another function such as SQR. Information within parentheses is called the function's "argument."

The only restriction so far as SQR is concerned, is that the computer cannot take the square root of a negative number. If you ask it to do so, an error message will be given at the time the program is being executed. Consider this example:

20 LET E = SQR (X)

If X should ever be negative during the time that the program is being run, the computer will give an error message and then take the square root of the positive form of X; thereafter continuing the program.

Here is a complete list of the built-in functions available in BASIC:

NAME	USE
SIN(X)	Compute sine of X
CØS(X)	Compute cosine of X
TAN(X)	Compute tangent of X
ATN(X)	Find arctangent of X
EXP(X)	Compute e^X
ABS(X)	Find absolute value of X
LOG(X)	Find natural logarithm of X
SQR(X)	Take square root of X
RND(X)	Get a random number
INT(X)	Extract largest integer of X

Some of these functions are self-explanatory. The first four are trigonometric functions; measurements are in radians.

The EXP function is used to compute the value of ''e'' (2.71828......) raised to the X power.

The ABS function gives the positive version of some number. For example, consider the value G in this BASIC statement.

10 LET A3 = ABS(G)

Suppose G has the value -3.7 when the statement is executed. The value of A3 will be set to 3.7 (the positive form of G). If G has the value 2.4, the value of A3 will be set to that positive value. G does not change.

When the LOG function is used, the log, to the base e, of the argument is given. A log cannot be taken of a negative value. As with the square root function, if the computer is asked to take the log of a negative value, the computer will print an error message, then take the log of the positive form of that number. The program will then continue from that point.

Let's show a few examples at this point:

equation	BASIC statement
$\alpha = \sin \beta$	20 LET A = SIN (B)
$x = \log_e (t + v)$	30 LET X = LØG (T + V)
$s = \sqrt{\cos t}$	40 LET S = SQR (CØS(T))
$m = e^{\sqrt{p}}$	50 LET M = EXP (SQR(P))

The RND function is a special BASIC function which gives a different random number between 0 and 1 each time that the function is called in a program. Here's a short illustrative program:

```
4000  LET  Z  =  RND (X)

4010  PRINT  Z

4020  GØ  TØ  4000

99999  END
```

Figure 8-1

When using RND, parentheses must be shown with a variable name within them. Though that argument has no real use, it is a technical requirement. The name X will always be OK.

The above program shows an endless loop during which random number after random number is requested. By actual test, thousands upon thousands of random numbers can be obtained without ever repeating a number.

As we've pointed out before, the above loop can be stopped at any time by the computer user. All he has to do is hit the letter P on the teletypewriter's keyboard while holding down CONTROL and SHIFT.

The INT function gives the largest whole number which can be found within some given value. For instance, consider this basic statement:

60 LET K = INT (H)

If H is 25.2, K will be set to 25; if H is 16.9, K will be 16; if H is .9824, K will be 0; if H is -2.4, K is -3, (not -2, as you might expect).

The INT function can be used to round numbers. Consider this example:

305 LET W = INT (S + .5)

If S is 4.2, S + .5 will be 4.7 and W will be set to 4; if S is 4.6, S + .5 will be 5.1, and W will be set to 5.

For negative numbers, .5 must still be added to the value to be rounded. For instance:

40 LET B = INT (C + .5)

If C is -2.2, C + .5 will be -1.7 and B will be set to -2. If C is -8.8, C + .5 will be -8.3 and B will be set to -9. As a point of interest, 8.5 rounds to 9 while -8.5 rounds to -8.

The INT and RND functions can team up to give a list of whole numbers which are equal to 0 or larger. It's done this way:

10 LET J = INT (10 * RND (X))

20 PRINT J

30 GØ TØ 10

99999 END

Figure 8-2

The numbers given by the *RND function are numbers like:

.43678
.05469
.74823
.55676
etc.

These same numbers, when acted upon by statements similar to the one at line 10, will print out as:

4
0
7
5
etc.

EXERCISES

Write these equations as BASIC statements:

$\emptyset = \Delta + \sqrt{\pi}$ (remember there are no Greek characters on the teletypewriter's keyboard)

$j = \sqrt{p + \sqrt{q}}$

$f = e^{t+4} - e^{t-4}$

$s = |t + u|$ (the absolute value of t + u is required)

$t = \sqrt{\sin k + \cos d}$

$d = \ln(f)$ (the natural log of f is required)

* See Lesson 24 for a description of RANDOMIZE.

Lesson 9

MAKING DECISIONS

You saw, in earlier lessons, BASIC statements which cause the computer to make decisions as it solves your problem. These are statements which begin with the word IF.

In this lesson, we'll explore the function of IF statements in more detail. Check this flow chart:

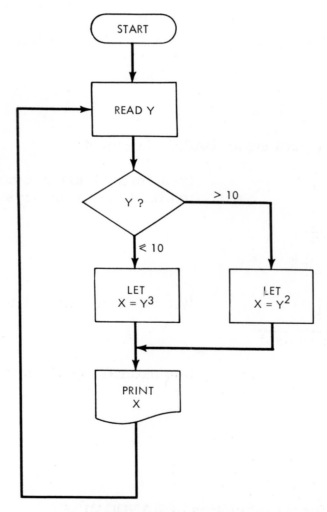

Figure 9-1

Now that you've had some practice working with flow charts, you ought to be able to see what has to be done here. In words, we want the computer to do this:

1. Read a value for Y (from the DATA statement).

2. Test the value. If it's greater than 10, have the computer set X equal to Y^2; if the value for Y is not greater than 10, have the computer set X equal to Y^3.

3. Print out the value of X. (It'll either be Y^2 or Y^3, of course).

4. Go back to read another value for Y, and repeat the procedure described above.

You'll spot the "loop" in the flow chart at once. This loop will be repeated over and over again, and will terminate only when the computer has used all numbers in the DATA statement.

Now, let's write out the program in BASIC:

```
50 READ Y

60 IF Y > 10 THEN 100

70 LET X = Y ↑ 3

80 PRINT X

90 GØ TØ 50

100 LET X = Y ↑ 2

110 GØ TØ 80

120 DATA 3, 6, 13, -4, 15, -2, 30, 10

99999 END
```

Figure 9-2

The statement at line number 60 contains a "conditional" branch. When the computer executes the statement, it looks at the value of Y, which the computer has read, and checks whether or not the condition mentioned in the statement is true. If it is true, the computer jumps to the line number mentioned in the statement. If it is not true, the computer goes to the next BASIC statement in sequence.

The first value for Y in this program is 3; since it is not greater than 10, the computer does not jump to line number 100. It goes instead to the next statement in the program. The next statement in this program, is of course, at line number 70.

Observe that by the use of IF and GO TO statements, the computer is forced to follow the paths shown in the flow chart. Note especially the placement of the GO TO statements at line numbers 90 and 110.

There will be 8 decisions made during the execution of this program. In three of the cases, the computer will go to the statement at line number 100; in five, it'll go to the statement at line number 70. When the computer runs out of data, it will stop.

The form of an IF statement must be written exactly as its pattern dictates. That pattern looks like this:

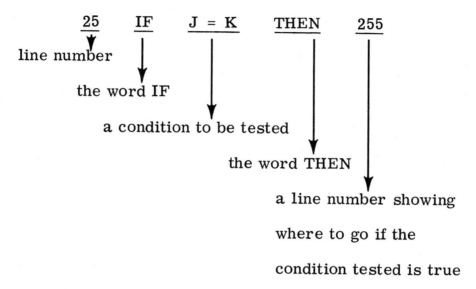

The condition to be tested always has three elements. Those elements are "subject," "object" and "relation." You'll be able to see those elements in the following condition:

$$J \quad > \quad K$$

The subject of the condition is J, the object is K and the relation is "greater than."

There are six possible BASIC relations. They are:

    =   equals
    >   greater than
    <   less than
    > = greater than or equal
    < = less than or equal
    < > not equal

These IF statements are all legal:

```
10 IF  L =  M  THEN  200
20 IF  Q <> W  THEN  300
30 IF  P <  R  THEN  400
40 IF  W >  T  THEN  500
50 IF  A > = E  THEN  600
60 IF  X < = Y  THEN  700
```

The word THEN must be shown in conditional statements. Don't write an IF statement like this:

```
470 IF  C = D  GØ TØ LINE 35
```

or this:

```
480 IF  E > F  THEN GØ TØ 80
```

In short, don't try writing IF statements that you think "ought to work." They won't unless you've followed the IF statement pattern exactly.   See Lesson 24 for a slight liberalization of this rule.

The subject and object of the conditions in an IF statement can be variable names, expressions or numbers. Here are some conditions which are OK:

$$W > = 7$$

$$A5 > ((B + C)/K) * (M + P)$$

$$S * (Q + P) = 14.3$$

$$7 - M5 <> R$$

$$16 < Z$$

$$T < = V$$

You can see that IF statements are very powerful, but they must be correctly used. Here is an incorrect way to use an IF statement. See if you can find what's logically wrong with this two-statement sequence:

```
40 IF   J = K THEN 50
50 LET M = N + P
```

If the value of J <u>does</u> equal the value of K, the computer will jump to line number 50 because the computer finds that the condition to be tested is true. Observe, though, that if J <u>does</u> <u>not</u> equal K, the computer goes to the same place.

Two or more IF statements can appear in sequence in a program. Let's consider a simple illustration. Suppose it is desired to determine which of three <u>different</u> positive values A, B, or C is largest. How would you compare the values against each other to arrive at a decision? Here's a flow chart you can use:

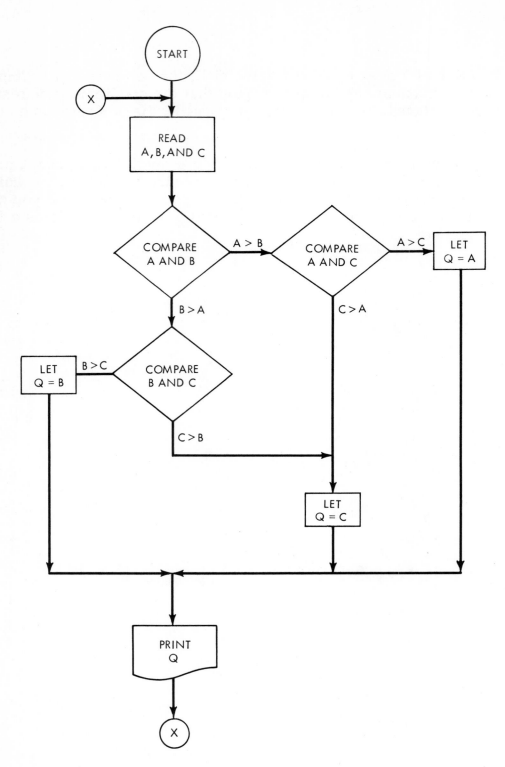

Figure 9-3

Since we're assuming all three values are different, there's no need to test for the "equals" conditions. Whenever a largest value is found, it is stored with the name Q; then that value is printed out. The computer is then instructed to go back and repeat the process. Again, as in previous examples, looping terminates when the computer runs out of numbers in the DATA statement.

Here's what the BASIC program, corresponding to the flow chart, looks like:

```
100 READ A, B, C
110 IF A > B THEN 300
120 IF B > C THEN 200
130 LET Q = C
140 PRINT Q
150 GØ TØ 100
200 LET Q = B
210 GØ TØ 140
300 IF A > C THEN 500
310 GØ TØ 130
500 LET Q = A
510 GØ TØ 140
520 DATA 3, 1, 4, 9, 2, 6, 7, 8, 2, 7, 6, 5, 1, 2, 3
99999 END
```

Figure 9-4

You will find it very instructive to follow the program case by case as the five sets of three values are read and processed in this program. The flow chart should also be consulted to see how the BASIC statements reflect the planning pictorially shown.

EXERCISE

Have the computer read a value from the program's DATA statement. Call the value V. If that value is 8.3, have the computer compute $X = V^3$ and have the computer print out the answer. Have the computer stop. If V does not equal 8.3, have the computer ignore V and go back to the program's READ statement to repeat the procedure.

Lesson 10

HAVING THE COMPUTER PRINT OUT ANSWERS

We've seen that where computer-type problems are to be solved, there are three steps involved:

1. Telling the computer what numbers are used in the program.

2. Telling the computer what to do with those numbers.

3. Having the computer print out the answer.

In previous lessons we've shown how the computer is told what numbers it is to use in a program, and how arithmetic is performed. In the last lesson you saw how conditional branches are made.

In this lesson we'll describe how you tell the computer to write out your answers. The PRINT statement is used. PRINT is very easy to use, yet it has some very powerful features. The easiest way to use PRINT is to write a statement such as this:

30 PRINT R

When the computer executes this statement, the value of R is printed out. Sometimes that answer will appear as:

145.6 or -92.3 or 55

but sometimes you'll see the answer as 1.54394E4 or -6.23466E-3.

You'll recognize the latter way of showing answers from our discussion of the exponential form. You can enter numbers into the computer in exponential form, and you can get back answers in that form.

The details regarding when you get one kind of answer versus another are these:

1. Up to six significant digits are printed using the letter E, unless the answers are exact whole numbers. In that case up to 9 digits are printed.

2. If a value is less than 0.1, it is printed in exponential (E) form unless the entire significant part of the answer can be expressed as a decimal number.

If you are not fussy about what kind of answers you get from your BASIC program, the rules shown above are not important. Sometimes, though, your report is to become some sort of permanent record. In that case, you'd like it to be as clear and attractive as possible.

If you want the computer to write out two or more answers on one line, the PRINT statement is written like this:

30 PRINT P, D, Q

When this statement is executed, the values of P, D and Q will be written out all on one line of the teletypewriter's paper.

Teletypewriter paper is divided into <u>five zones</u> of 15 character positions each. When you ask for one answer, that answer begins at column 1 of the paper; if you ask for two answers, the numbers start at columns 1 and 16; three answers, columns 1, 16, and 31, etc.

In general then, only five answers are possible per line. There's an exception to this rule which we'll mention shortly, but we recommend you don't fiddle with it just yet. It's likely to get you into trouble.

If you write:

30 PRINT A, B, C, D, E, F, G

you will get five answers on one line and two on the next.

Suppose you want the computer to write out some sort of message like "ERROR IN DATA". Write your PRINT statement like this:

85 PRINT "ERRØR IN DATA"

Whatever you show within quotation marks will be printed exactly as you show it. This feature makes it easy for you to set up program headings and column headings for your program. For instance, consider this example:

```
10 PRINT "THIS PRØGRAM CALCULATES SINES"

20 PRINT

30 PRINT "RADIAN VALUE   SINE"

40 PRINT

99999 END
```

Figure 10-1

When these statements are executed, the computer will print the first message on the teletypewriter paper. The message has 29 characters (including spaces) and it will appear in columns 1 through 29 of the paper.

Then the computer will skip one line. (That's what the single word PRINT does at line number 20.)

Next, the computer will print the column headings RADIAN VALUE and SINE. The word RADIAN will appear beginning in column 1 of the teletype-writer paper, and the word SINE will appear beginning in column 16. (There are three spaces between the word VALUE and the word SINE.)

In PRINT lines you can mix variable names and messages within quotes. For instance, this PRINT statement is OK.

16 PRINT "VALUE ØF ALPHA IS", A

When the computer executes this statement, it will print the message VALUE OF ALPHA IS beginning in column 1. The value of A will be printed beginning in column 31. The quoted message extends into the second zone (it's longer than 15 characters); the value of A, therefore, will begin in the third zone.

If the comma separating the quoted message from the variable name A had been left out, the value of A would have begun in the second zone immediately after the quoted message was written. It's a good idea to use commas to separate the various elements of a PRINT statement.

There's no limit to the kind, number, or order of elements in a PRINT statement. This example is just one simple way of writing a PRINT statement:

24 PRINT "A=", A, "B=", B, "C=", C, "D=", D

A valuable feature of the PRINT statement is the fact that elements can be expressions. Consider this example:

510 PRINT "VALUE OF RHØ =", (R3 * R4)/(K - H)

When the statement is executed, the computer calculates $\dfrac{R3 \times R4}{K - H}$ and prints out the answer following the message VALUE OF RHØ.

This way of doing things is equivalent to using these statements:

500 LET R = (R3 * R4)/(K - H)
510 PRINT "VALUE OF RHØ =", R

The advantage of using the former method is that one BASIC statement is eliminated. The disadvantage is that if R is needed later in the program, it can't be used because it was never stored. The latter method, of course, sets up a computer location called R with the value $\dfrac{R3 \times R4}{K - H}$ and that value can be used later in the program.

If more than 5 answers are required on the teletypewriter paper, the semicolon (;) can be used in place of the comma. As many as six, eight, ten, even up to eleven, numbers can be printed per line. Here's how you'd write the PRINT statement:

400 PRINT A; B; C; D; E; F; G; H

The results you get from a statement of this type are difficult to predict. We'd suggest you do some experimenting if you have an application requiring packing as many answers as possible per line.

Lesson 10

If a PRINT statement is within the statements of a loop, you may write it like this:

20 PRINT X,   or   20 PRINT X;

The computer will <u>not</u> automatically advance to the next line after printing X. It'll wait for the next time that the PRINT statement is executed, then print the next value of X on the same line. In like manner, the computer keeps printing X values on the same line until there is no more room on the line. Then the computer goes to a new line position for additional X values.

See Lesson 24 for the TAB feature of PRINT.

While we are on the subject of writing messages, let's get acquainted with the REM statement. REM lets you place remarks at strategic points in your program, which tell what is going on in various sections of the program. Those remarks are <u>not printed during the execution</u> of the program, but they appear when you list it. Here's an example:

```
10 REM READ VALUES FØR ALPHA AND BETA

20 REM

30 REM

40 INPUT A, B

50 REM    SUM VALUES AND PRINT ANSWER

60 PRINT A + B

80 IF A+B = 0 THEN 500

90 GØ TØ 20

500 STØP

99999 END
```

Figure 10-2

Lesson 11

ARRAYS AND SUBSCRIPTS

Suppose you have 4 costs associated with the manufacture of flimflams in your plant. These costs are:

1. Cost of components purchased

2. Cost of components manufactured

3. Cost of labor

4. Cost of overhead

Suppose you need a program which will add up these costs and print them out. One way to do this is to give each cost a name, then have the computer add them up using this statement:

$$10 \text{ LET } T = C1 + C2 + C3 + C4$$

C1, C2, C3 and C4 are the four costs involved. When the statement is executed each of the names has an associated value, and these are added together giving T.

This way of handling individual data items is often satisfactory, but sometimes it can be awkward to deal with. There is another way of working with related data items. That way is to set aside groups of computer locations all with the same name. That name must be a <u>single character</u> such as A, B, X, etc. The DIM statement is used to do this.

Let's examine this illustrative program:

Lesson 11

```
10 DIM  C(4)

20 READ  C(1),  C(2),  C(3),  C(4)

30 LET  T = C(1) + C(2) + C(3) + C(4)

40 PRINT T

50 DATA 147.56,  234.20,  764.23,  94.75

99999 END
```

Figure 11-1

At line number 10 you see a statement which sets aside four computer locations all called C. The letters DIM are an abbreviation for "dimension." (We're showing that the "dimension" of C is 4. That is, there are four C's.) Later you'll see that actually 5 locations are set up when you write "4," but ignore that technicality for now.

Notice how one C is differentiated from another. At line number 20 we see that C(1) means "the first C;" C(2) means "the second C;" etc.

Use of the DIM statement in a program establishes an "array." By "array" is meant a group of locations all with the same name. Another word for array is "table," a term that many people prefer.

You can show which element of an array is to be used by writing the name of the array, then showing a number within parentheses. That number shows which element of the array is called for.

For example, the statement:

20 LET Q(3) = 9.2

means that the third Q is to be given the value 9.2.

In Figure 11-1 above, the element C(1) of the array C is set to 147.56; C(2) is set to 234.20; C(3) is set to 764.23; and C(4) is set to 94.75.

Lesson 11

At line 30, these four values are added together, and at line number 40, the sum is printed out.

The number shown within parentheses, following the name of an array, is called a "subscript." A subscript's purpose is to show which data item of a table of data items is to be used.

A subscript can be a whole number like 5, 6, 13, 20, or a variable name such as I, J, S, V.

These subscripts are OK, for instance, in a program using an array called P:

```
100 LET  P(3) = 2.6
200 LET  P(K) = 4.7
300 LET  T = P(L) + P(2)
```

Since K and L are used as subscripts in the brief example, those names must have been given values earlier in the program. Otherwise the computer wouldn't know which elements of the P array are to be referenced.

Suppose K has been set to 6, earlier in the program, and L has been set to 8. Now P(K) and P(L) would have meanings.

A subscript must always be a whole number, of course. In the previous example, if K is a mixed number, the fractional part of the number will be dropped. There is no rounding.

Suppose K has been set to 4.6. The subscript for P in this next statement would be 4:

```
810 LET  P(K) = 2.4
```

It will be the 4th P which is set to 2.4.

Subscripts must never be negative. They can be 0 (zero) or any positive whole number. See Lesson 24 about zero subscripts soon to become illegal.

Subscripts can be computed. Consider this example:

```
50 LET  P((K6-3) / (4 * Q2)) = 8.7
```

The subscript for P is perfectly legal. The computation within parentheses is made and a whole number generated. This number will act as the subscript for P.

Suppose K6 equals 43 and Q2 equals 2. The value of the subscript will be (43-3) / (4 x 2) or 40/8 = 5.

No matter how complicated the calculation shown as a subscript, it can always be computed. It is expected, however, that the computation results in a non-negative whole number equal to zero or greater.

A subscript must never be larger than the maximum number of elements in an array, as specified by the DIM statement.

A DIM statement showing the name and size of an array can be written anywhere in a BASIC program so long as it appears before any element of the array is used.

The name of an array must be a single letter like P or X or C. An array name such as R6, B2, or A6 is illegal. Subscripts, on the other hand, can use any legal BASIC names. The names H3, P2, and Y8 can be used directly as subscripts or within calculations helping to make up subscripts.

The DIM statement is not needed if the array has 11 or fewer elements. Recall that the first element of an array is the zero'th one. This means that if your DIM statement looks like this:

10 DIM R(50)

you're actually setting aside 51 (not 50) computer locations all called R. You can reference R(0) in your programming. You may write a DIM statement even if, technically, it isn't needed.

The point at which you must set up a DIM statement for an array is where you need an array having 12 or more items. Here's an example of an array composed of twelve elements.

40 DIM E(11)

The largest number you can show in a DIM statement, is 1022. Thus, by writing this:

$$60 \ \text{DIM} \ G(1022)$$

you set aside 1023 locations all called G.

Possibly a great deal of what we've said in this lesson seems to have little application. You may be right. It all depends upon what you're trying to do in your program.

Reserve your decision whether arrays are useful or not until after you've studied the next lesson giving details of the FOR and NEXT statements.

EXERCISE

Explain in your own words what this BASIC program segment does.

```
10 DIM X(100)

20 READ X(6), X(8)

30 LET K3 = X(6) * X(8)

40 PRINT K3
      :  ⎫
      :  ⎬  Statements not shown
      :  ⎭
100 DATA 4.3, 7.4, 8.9, 7.6, 2.3, -6.3

99999 END
```

Figure 11-2

Lesson 12

LOOPS

Now you will see how just a few instructions can cause the computer to do a great deal of work. You can have the computer "loop." You've already seen loops in earlier lessons; in this lesson we'll discuss them in detail.

Here is a loop:

20 GØ TØ 30

30 GØ TØ 20

99999 END

Figure 12-1

This is a complete BASIC program. You can see, though, that it is a "do nothing" program. Nothing useful is being accomplished. The computer will keep jumping from one instruction to the other indefinitely, or until you stop the program by hitting S on the teletypewriter's keyboard.

Loops are, of course, more useful than the one shown above. Here is a more reasonable one:

```
10 READ R

20 LET C = 2 * 3.1416 * R

30 PRINT C, R

40 GØ TØ 10

50 DATA 2.4, 6.7, 8.3, 9, 6.7, 8, 3.4

99999 END
```

Figure 12-2

In this example, the computer reads from the DATA statement, value after value of R. After each value of R is read, the computer calculates the circumference, C, of a circle and prints it. The value of R is also printed. You'll notice that the computer goes back to line number 10 over and over again. This will happen until there are no more data values to be read from the DATA statement.

Suppose you knew ahead of time exactly how many data items will <u>always</u> be in the DATA statement, say 12. Now you can write a "loop" using the special loop statements FOR and NEXT. It's done this way:

```
20 FØR I = 1 TØ 12

30 READ R

40 LET C = 2 * 3.1416 * R

50 PRINT C, R

60 NEXT I

70 STØP

80 DATA 4.2, 3, 7.6, 4.7, 8, 7.2, 9, 8.3, 3.2, 1.1, 3, 2.1

99999 END
```

Figure 12-3

Study the statement at line number 20. What does it mean? It means simply, "execute all the BASIC statements which follow, up to and including the statement which reads NEXT I." Notice that the name I is mentioned in the FOR statement appearing at line number 20. Observe also the location of the statement reading NEXT I. It appears at line number 60.

The important point to note here is that the statements which are to be executed, are to be executed not once but several times. How many times? The answer is 12. That's what "I = 1 to 12" means in line 20.

The form of a FOR statement is this: the word FOR is followed by a name, an equal sign, and two other numbers separated by the word TO. Thusly:

20 FØR I = 1 TØ 12

What happens is this: a counter is set up. The name of the counter is the variable name which appears in the FOR statement.

In the example given, the name of the counter is I, but it can be any legal variable name. This means that such names as A, C7, H9, can act as counter names.

The series of statements which are to be executed over and over in the above illustration, are the ones which appear at line numbers 30, 40, 50 and 60. The first time that the series is executed, the counter is set at 1. When the computer sees the statement at line number 60 (NEXT I), the computer increments the value of the counter by 1. The value of the counter will then be 2. The counter is tested to see if it exceeds 12. If it does, the loop is terminated, if it does not, the computer executes statements 30, 40, 50 and 60 again.

This procedure will continue until the counter has reached, and actually used, the value 12. When that happens, the statements in the loop will have been executed exactly 12 times.

The computer will know that it has executed those statements the correct number of times and will stop doing so. The computer will then go to the statement in the program which follows the NEXT statement. In this example, that statement is located at line number 70.

Look again at the FOR statement. The statement shows the initial and final values of the counter used. The initial value does not have to be 1. It can be any number that the program requires.

To review, when the counter's value reaches the final value mentioned in the FOR statement, the loop's statements are executed while the counter holds that final value. Then the computer "escapes" from the loop. It goes to the next sequential statement following the NEXT statement.

FOR and NEXT statements form pairs. Whenever there's a FOR statement, there will also be a NEXT statement naming the same counter. FOR appears at the beginning of a loop, NEXT appears at the end of the loop.

These are legitimate FOR statements:

```
FØR L3 = 1 TØ 30
FØR K  = 1 TØ 15
FØR Q  = 5 TØ 20
FØR R3 = 7 TØ 50
```

The first FOR shows that the name L3 is to vary from 1 through 30; the second FOR shows that K is to vary from 1 through 15. In the next two FOR statements, the values of the counters will vary from 5 through 20 and from 7 through 50 respectively.

The number of times that the loops will be executed in the last two FOR statements are 16 and 44 respectively. Does this look like once too many for each loop? It isn't. The initial setting is shown and the final setting is shown. The number of iterations is therefore one more than you might at first suppose.

Here is the "outline" of a FOR loop

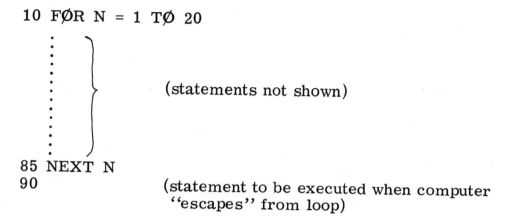

10 FØR N = 1 TØ 20

(statements not shown)

85 NEXT N
90   (statement to be executed when computer "escapes" from loop)

See if you can answer these questions about the above loop:

1. What is the name of the counter?

2. What will be the value of the counter during the time that the statements in the loop are being executed for the 10th time?

3. What will be the value of the counter during the time that the statements in the loop are being executed for the last time?

4. Where will the computer go after looping has been completely executed?

There is no limitation to the number of statements which may appear between the FOR statement and the NEXT statement. You may have only one, fifty, one-hundred or more as required.

The two numbers in the FOR statement can be any values you choose, negative or positive. For example, these FOR statements are OK:

```
50 FØR K = -10 TØ 15
75 FØR L = -60 TØ -45
85 FØR P3 = 0 TØ 50
90 FØR R9 = -40 TØ 0
```

The "step size" in each case is 1. This means that when the counter is incremented, the increment is always 1.

Step sizes other than 1 are permissible. Look at this FOR statement:

```
500 FØR W = 20 TØ 40 STEP 2
```

The increment for W in this case is 2. The values which W will hold are 20, 22, 24, etc. Increments of 3, 4, 5 or more are OK. Example:

```
600 FØR X = 10 TØ 20 STEP 3
```

A counter will never hold a value larger than a terminating value shown; in this example, 20. The counter X will hold the values 10, 13, 16, and 19 (but not 22).

Now look at these step sizes:

```
60 FØR I = 3.5 TØ 10 STEP .35
70 FØR J = 0 TØ 50.1 STEP 1.6
80 FØR P = -10 TØ -3 STEP 3
90 FØR Q = -50 TØ -100 STEP -2
```

These are OK. You'd better be careful when you use unusual beginning and ending values for the counter or for step sizes. Don't write a FOR statement which cannot possibly be executed. For example, this FOR statement is impossible:

```
75 FØR R = 10 TØ 50 STEP -10
```

Do you see what's wrong? An increment of -10 for R will keep decreasing R's value rather than increasing it. The values of R will be 10, 0, -10, -20, etc.

Similarly:

85 FØR T = -40 TØ -100 STEP 10

will change T in the wrong direction. The values of T will be -40, -30, -20, etc.

These last two statements would cause non-terminating loops. The computer will not accept such statements, giving you error messages.

When step sizes are not mentioned, they are assumed to be 1. It's OK to write "STEP 1" if you want to. Most people leave that standard step size out, though.

The numbers mentioned in a FOR statement can be symbolic or equations. These statements are OK:

300 FØR Z1 = P TØ L STEP J
400 FØR Z2 = B TØ C STEP -D
500 FØR Z3 = P * 3 TØ (C + D) / 2 STEP 5 * J

Values for P, L, J, B, C and D must, of course, exist when these kinds of statements are executed. Those values can be read from DATA statements or computed earlier in the program.

There's more to the art of looping. We'll continue this discussion in the next lesson.

EXERCISE

What's wrong with these FOR statements:

410 FØR K = 1 THRU 10

620 FØR PD = 10 TØ 99

98 FØR 3X = 10 TØ 40 STEP -5

25 FØR S = 25, 35 STEP .5

15 FØR S FROM 5 TØ 25

Lesson 13

LOOPS (CONTINUED)

Loops have many uses. We've shown you some examples but there are many others. Here's an instructive example. Suppose you want to add up these numbers:

$$1 + 2 + 3 + 4 + 5 \ldots \ldots \ldots + 100$$

There's an equation which gives this answer but let's overlook it for now. (The equation is $S = \dfrac{N^2 + N}{2}$ where S is the sum and N is the largest number in the list.)

Here's one way you can write the BASIC program to solve the problem:

```
10 LET S = 0

20 FØR I = 1 TØ 100

30 LET S = S + I

40 NEXT I

50 PRINT S

99999 END
```

Figure 13-1

You will note that previous to the loop statements, we set aside a computer location called S. You will see the reason for this as we explore the functioning of the loop. Note that the FOR statement says: "execute the statements which follow the FOR statement up to and including the statement at line number 40." (That's where the NEXT statement is.)

The computer is directed to execute these statements one hundred times. The first time the statements are executed, the initial value of S will be zero; the value of I will be one. The new value of S will be one. That is, zero plus one equals one. The computer will see the NEXT statement and will know that it has to go back and execute the statements which follow the FOR statement again.

The second time that the statements following the FOR statement are executed, the initial value of S will be one, the value of I will be two. The sum of S and I will be three, and this result will become the new value for S. When the computer again sees the statement at line 40, it will examine the value of I to see whether it has been used with the value one hundred yet. If it has not, the computer will branch back to execute the statements following the FOR statement again.

This same procedure continues over and over again with I increasing by one each time. Finally, when I equals one hundred, and has been used with that value, the computer will stop executing those statements and will drop down into the statement at line number 50. The statement at line 50 causes the computer to print out the value of S, which now contains the answer to the problem.

In this example you have seen that the counter, I, actually provides two functions. It acts as a counter, which tells the computer when it must stop executing the loop. Further, the current value of the counter may be used in calculations at any time. This is shown in the statement which follows the FOR statement, where S is being set with the value S + I. Whatever the value of I is, at the time the statement is executed, the value will be added to the current value of S, and the result will be the new value of S.

You'll recall that when we explained the meaning of the equals sign in BASIC statements, we said the meaning is this:

"make the calculation shown on the right-hand side of the equals sign and place the result of the calculation at the location named on the left-hand side of the equals sign."

This means that such BASIC statements as:

$$10 \ \text{LET} \ P = P + I$$

and

$$50 \ \text{LET} \ K = K + 3$$

are perfectly legal.

Of course these statements are OK too:

```
400 LET B = 3.9
410 LET J = 99.9
420 LET Q8 = 6
```

though there are no real "calculations" shown at the right-hand side of the equals sign. The values 3.9, 99.9 and 6 are set in locations B, J and Q8 respectively.

In Figure 13-1, you may have wondered about the statement at line number 10, "LET S = 0." Is it really necessary to set S to an initial value of zero. The answer is no. You can depend upon S having an initial value of zero before the program begins. However, setting S to zero is good "initializing" practice and it doesn't hurt to do it. For instance, if you were concerned with summing several series of numbers, not just one, you'd have to reset S to zero before working on a new series.

Here's another example which shows a counter being used both as a counter and as an actual value in the program:

```
10 FØR N = 1 TØ 20

20 PRINT N

30 NEXT N

99999 END
```

Figure 13-2

This program will cause twenty numbers to be written out. The numbers will be on twenty lines and will be 1, 2, 3, 4, etc., through 20.

The values of counters can also be used as subscripts. Before reading the following discussion, review chapter 11 which tells about setting up arrays and what subscripts are.

Let's look at this program:

```
10 DIM X(30)

20 FØR L = 1 TØ 10

30 LET X(L) = 0

40 NEXT L

50 FØR L = 11 TØ 20

60 LET X(L) = 1

70 NEXT L

80 FØR L = 21 TØ 30

90 LET X(L) = 2

100 NEXT L

99999 END
```

Figure 13-3

In this example you will notice there have been thirty X locations set aside in the computer. (Actually 31, if you count the "zeroth" location.) We are writing three FOR loops. The first loop will set the first ten X locations to the value "0"; the second loop will set the second ten X locations to the value "1"; the third loop will set the third set of ten X locations to the value "2."

You will notice that the counter we are using here is called L. In the first FOR loop, L is being made to vary from one through ten. In the second loop, L is being made to vary from eleven through twenty, and in the third loop, L is being made to vary from twenty-one through thirty. This will account for all thirty X locations.

We have used the name, L, in all three loops. However, it is not necessary to use the same counter name for all loops. We could have used a different name for each loop. The next example shows that we may use different names for the counter, and that the locations X may be set to the values we require in any order:

```
10 DIM X(30)

20 FØR J = 11 TØ 20

30 LET X(J) = 1

40 NEXT J

50 FØR K2 = 1 TØ 10

60 LET X(K2) = 0

70 NEXT K2

80 FØR M = 21 TØ 30

90 LET X(M) = 2

100 NEXT M

99999 END
```

Figure 13-4

A few moments study of these loops will show that we have used the name J, in one place; the name K2, in another place; and the name M, in a third place. It is <u>not necessary</u> to set all values in an array. Arrays can be dimensioned larger than actually required.

In the example, we did not follow any definite order when we set the locations X to the values that we required. The first loop, for example, set the eleventh through twentieth X locations to the value "1"; the second loop set the first through tenth X locations to the value "0," and the third loop set the twenty-first through thirtieth X locations to the value "2."

Incidentally, the program shown in Figure 13-4 simply illustrates how subscripts can be used in a loop. The program is really an exercise in futility. It doesn't do anything useful. There isn't even one PRINT statement in the program.

To summarize, a counter in a FOR statement can have three uses. They are:

              1. A simple counter.

              2. An actual value in equations.

              3. A subscript.

Loops are very useful in programs. It's possible to have loops within loops and even loops within those loops. The next lesson will discuss double subscripts and loops within loops.

EXERCISE

What are the three uses for the counter in a FOR statement:

1.

2.

3.

Show three very simple BASIC programs (5 or 6 statements maximum) illustrating the three uses mentioned above.

Lesson 14

LOOPS WITHIN LOOPS

We touched upon subscripting in previous lessons. You noticed that when we subscript variables with a name (20 LET X(J) = 0, for example), we can riffle through a large number of variables easily by using the FOR and NEXT statements. We've seen that whenever variables are to be subscripted you <u>must</u> write a DIM statement if the number of elements to be shown in the <u>DIM</u> statement is 11 or larger. Example:

20 DIM X (1000)

30 FØR L = 1 TØ 1000

40 LET X (L) = 0

60 NEXT L

99999 END

Figure 14-1

One thousand X locations were set aside in the computer with the DIM statement.

DIM statements can have another form in BASIC.

Here it is:

50 DIM X (5, 4)

This sets up an area in the computer's memory which may be <u>thought of</u> as looking like this:

Lesson 14

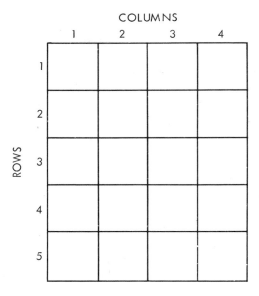

COLUMNS

Figure 14-2

Therefore, X(5,4) means 20 X locations arranged in rectangular form with five rows and 4 columns. (Actually, 6 x 5 or 30 locations are set up because there is a zero'th row and a zero'th column always given by 2-dimensional DIM statements, but <u>in this lesson</u>, <u>we'll</u> <u>ignore</u> the extra row and column.)

If you write the following statement:

80 LET X(3,2) = 10

the X location you are referring to is in the <u>3rd row</u> and the <u>2nd column</u>. This one:

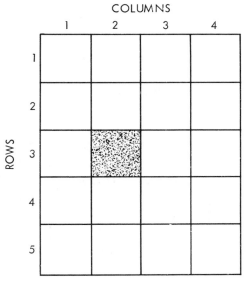

Figure 14-3

In the statement, the information shown within parentheses is a subscript. It's a double subscript, though, as distinguished from the single subscripts we showed in earlier lessons. X is an array and whenever any element of the array is referenced, its subscript must have two parts.

The subscript in a doubly-subscripted array, then, will refer to a variable at its row and column location. That is:

90 LET X(5,4) = 30   (5th row, 4th column)

references this X location:

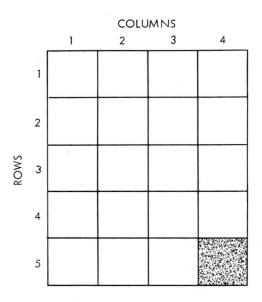

Figure 14-4

You can think of an array as being set up in rectangular form but actually, within the computer's memory, the elements are strung out in consecutive order. This fact does not have to concern you because whenever
you mention a doubly-subscripted array's element, you can picture it as
being in some row and some column.

You can use two-part subscripts in these ways:

```
510 LET X(3,4) = 1.5
520 LET X(I,5) = 2.4
530 LET X(7,Q) = -8
540 LET X(I,J) = 92.4
550 LET X(S + 6, V*W) = 2.1
```

Note that at line 550, two parts of the subscript are shown, but each part shows a calculation. Calculated subscripts are all right, and the calculations can be as complicated as required. The results of the calculations should, of course, be positive whole numbers. (Zero subscripts are OK too if you're using the zero'th row and/or column.)

It goes without saying that in the above examples, when the statements at line numbers 510 through 550 are executed, the names I, Q, J, S, V and W should have been given values earlier in the program.

We can now talk about loops within loops. They have the form shown by this outline:

```
10 FØR B = 1 TØ 5
        .
        .
        .
80 FØR C = 1 TØ 3
        .
        .
        .
150 NEXT C
        .
        .
        .
200 NEXT B
```

Dotted areas indicate BASIC statements not shown.

This example has two loops; an inner and an outer. The inner loop is controlled by the counter C and the outer by the counter B.

When the loops first begin to be executed, B will be set to 1 and statements will be executed down to where the second loop begins. There, C will be set to 1 and execution of the program will continue down to line number 150 where NEXT C is located. At that point the computer branches back to the beginning of the inner loop where C will be set to two. The statements of the inner loop will be executed again down to line number 150 while C equals 2 and B remains constant at 1.

This process will continue once more (with C set to 3, at which point the inner loop will be completed), and execution will continue past line number 150 down to line number 200. But this will represent execution only once through the outer loop; a branch will then be made back to the beginning of the outer loop.

B will be set to 2, and execution will again proceed toward the inner loop statement.

Every time that the inner loop is encountered, it has to be re-initialized and completed. That is, C will have to be set to 1, 2 and 3 before an "escape" out of that loop can be made. This means that the statements within the inner loop will be executed 3 x 5 times or 15 times.

This tabulation shows how the outer and inner counters change as the computer executes these loops:

```
B = 1
C = 1          outer loop executed first time
C = 2
C = 3
B = 2
C = 1          outer loop executed second time
C = 2
C = 3
B = 3
C = 1          outer loop executed third time
C = 2
C = 3
B = 4
C = 1          outer loop executed fourth time
C = 2
C = 3
B = 5
C = 1          outer loop executed fifth time
C = 2
C = 3
```

We can use the loop-within-loop idea to set to "fifty" all elements of a doubly-subscripted array. Study this example:

```
10 DIM A(3,4)

20 FØR I = 1 TØ 3

30 FØR J = 1 TØ 4

40 LET A(I,J) = 50

50 NEXT J

60 NEXT I
```

Figure 14-5

Lesson 14

The first time through the equation at line 40, LET A(I,J) = 50, the values of I and J are 1 and 1 respectively. The effect is the same as if the equation at line number 40 had been written:

40 LET A(1,1) = 50

J will be increased to 2, then 3, then 4, while I remains at 1. Then I will advance to 2 and J will cycle again through 1, 2, 3 and 4.

Finally I will advance to 3; J will cycle through 1, 2, 3 and 4 and both loops will have been completed. The last values of I and J will be 3 and 4 respectively. The effect will be as if the equation at line number 40 had been written:

40 LET A(3,4) = 50

You'll note that every possible combination of subscripts for the A array will have been used, thus setting every element of the array to fifty. No element will have been accessed more than once.

Don't worry about why we've set every element of the A array to fifty. Why we do certain things depends upon what the problem is. What we want you to see from these illustrations is how every element of an array is accessed in a systematic way. There is a more practical example of array usage near the end of this lesson.

It's all right for your program to exit from a loop conditionally (by use of an IF statement). If the program must re-enter the loop, use a "GO TO" referencing the line number of the loop's NEXT statement. The counter will automatically be incremented by the step size and the loop will resume.

You can write loops within loops, and even other loops within those loops, but different counter names must be used for loops within loops.

Loops within loops must not "overlap." You can write loops like this, for example:

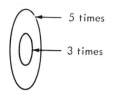

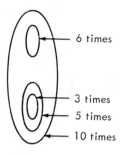

Figure 14-6

But this kind of loop is illegal:

Figure 14-7

In other words, don't try to set up a loop within a loop this way:

100 DIM B(5, 3)

200 F$\emptyset$R I = 1 T$\emptyset$ 5

300 F$\emptyset$R J = 1 T$\emptyset$ 3

⎫
⎬   Statements not
⎭   shown

600 NEXT I

700 NEXT J

Figure 14-8

This is illegal overlapping. Reverse the statements at line numbers 600 and 700 and you'll be OK.

Suppose we have two sets of resistors. Set 1 consists of resistors A_1 A_2 A_3 and A_4. Set 2 consists of resistors B_1 B_2 B_3. It is desired to see what the effective resistances are of A resistors and B resistors connected in parallel like this:

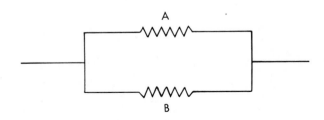

Figure 14-9

Let's have the computer calculate 12 answers. Hold A_1 constant while varying the B resistors from B_1 to B_3. Then hold A_2 constant while varying B from B_1 to B_3, etc.

You'll recall that the equation for parallel resistors is:

$$t = \frac{a \text{ x } b}{a + b}$$

Where t is the resistance, and a and b are the resistors in parallel. A program to give us the 12 answers required is this:

```
10 DIM A(4), B(3), T(4,3)

20 INPUT A(1), A(2), A(3), A(4)

30 INPUT B(1), B(2), B(3)

40 FØR I = 1 TØ 4

50 FØR J = 1 TØ 3

60 LET T(I,J) = (A(I) * B(J)) / (A(I) + B(J))

70 NEXT J

80 NEXT I

90 PRINT T(1,1), T(1,2), T(1,3)

100 PRINT T(2,1), T(2,2), T(2,3)

110 PRINT T(3,1), T(3,2), T(3,3)

120 PRINT T(4,1), T(4,2), T(4,3)

300 GØ TØ 20

99999 END
```

Figure 14-10

This is not the only way to solve this problem. You're welcome to improve it. The answers, using our method, will have this form:

$$A_1B_1 \qquad A_1B_2 \qquad A_1B_3$$

$$A_2B_1 \qquad A_2B_2 \qquad A_2B_3$$

$$A_3B_1 \qquad A_3B_2 \qquad A_3B_3$$

$$A_4B_1 \qquad A_4B_2 \qquad A_4B_3$$

Figure 14-11

The reader should experiment with this program varying output formats, putting in column headings, etc.

Incidentally, the DIM statement for this illustrative program is not necessary since the numbers shown in the statements are less than 11.

If you do much work with data values in matrix form, you'll enjoy lesson 15 which tells about several matrix operations available in BASIC. You may skip the lesson if you don't use matrices.

EXERCISE

Write the outline of FOR and NEXT statements to illustrate these loops. Show only those statements. Use dotted lines to indicate BASIC statements not shown:

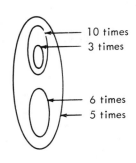

10 times
3 times
6 times
5 times

Lesson 15

MATRIX COMPUTATIONS

There are eleven special BASIC statement types especially designed for matrix computations. Using these statements a person can add, subtract and multiply matrices as well as manipulate them in other ways.

The eleven matrix instructions all begin with the letters MAT. A simple example of what one MAT instruction looks like is this one:

20 MAT A = B * C

This statement will cause the matrix B to be multiplied by the matrix C, and the result assigned to the matrix A.

All matrices named in MAT statements <u>must</u> be <u>defined</u> using <u>DIM statements.</u> The only detail to keep in mind when defining a matrix is that matrices have one more element in each dimension than the figures shown in the DIM statement. Example:

10 DIM A (3, 3)

The statement shows that A is a 4 x 4 matrix. It has 4 rows and 4 columns. The rows and columns are numbered 0, 1, 2 and 3 respectively. Be sure to read Lesson 24 covering extended BASIC. The zero'th element in each direction is being eliminated.

In the DIM statement, the first number applies to the number of rows the matrix has and the second number applies to the number of columns it has. Thus:

35 DIM P (4, 5)

Lesson 15

means the matrix P has 5 rows and 6 columns. The rows are numbered 0, 1, 2, 3, 4; the columns are numbered 0, 1, 2, 3, 4, 5.

When selecting a name for a matrix, you may use only a single letter. Such names as A3, P4, etc. are not legal as matrix names.

You can always calculate the number of elements in a matrix by multiplying the number of rows by the number of columns. In this example:

50 DIM Q(5, 6)

there are 42 elements of the array Q (6 rows, 7 columns).

You may define an array larger than one you actually intend to use in a program. Its exact dimensions can be read from a DATA statement at the time you run the program. Here's an example:

10 DIM X (15, 15), Y (15, 15), Z (15, 15)

20 READ I, J

30 MAT READ X(I, J), Y(I, J)

$\left.\begin{array}{c} \vdots \\ \vdots \\ \vdots \\ \vdots \\ \vdots \end{array}\right\}$ Statements not shown

150 DATA 2, 3

160 DATA 1, 2, 3, 4, 5, 6, 7, 8, 9, 10, 11, 12

170 DATA 0, 1, 2, 3, -1, 0, 1, 2, 1, 1, 0, 0

99999 END

Figure 15-1

At line number 10 matrices are set up with maximum dimensions. At line number 20, the values for I and J are read from a DATA statement. Note that I and J are shown in the MAT READ instruction at line number 30.

MAT READ is one of the eleven matrix instructions we'll be introducing in this lesson. Its function here is to take values from DATA statements until 12 values have been loaded into matrix X and 12 values into matrix Y.

Observe that I gets the value 2 and J gets the value 3. When I and J are used at line 30, they designate 3 rows and 4 columns of values. The product of 3 times 4 is 12.

The values for the 3 x 4 X matrix will be read in as follows:

1	2	3	4
5	6	7	8
9	10	11	12

The 3 x 4 Y matrix will be read in as follows:

0	1	2	3
-1	0	1	2
1	1	0	0

The complete list of MAT instructions include these: (the matrix names shown are examples).

```
MAT  READ  P,  Q,  R,  Z
MAT  PRINT  X,  Y
MAT  A = B + C
MAT  D = E - F
MAT  G = H * J
MAT  K = INV (L)
MAT  M = TRN (N)
MAT  S = (2) * T
MAT  U = ZER
MAT  V = CØN
MAT  W = IDN
```

READ

A matrix is loaded from numbers shown in DATA statements. Here are some ways that READ can be used:

```
10  MAT  READ  P (K, M)
50  MAT  READ  Q (2, 3)
75  MAT  READ  R (I + 3, 4),  Z (N, 3 * J)
80  MAT  READ  T
```

The names K, M, I, N, and J must have been assigned values when these matrix READ statements are executed. Don't forget that DIM statements must be shown for matrices P, Q, R and T. In the last example, the entire matrix, as specified by its DIM statement, will be read.

PRINT

This instruction prints out the matrices named with the dimensions previously assigned. Here are some ways to show PRINT:

```
200  MAT  PRINT  X
210  MAT  PRINT  X, Y
220  MAT  PRINT  X; Y
```

Lesson 15

Values will be printed 5 numbers per line except where ";" is shown. The X matrix above using ";" will be printed tightly packed.

ADDITION

Matrices can be added. Example:

150 MAT A = B + C

(B is added to C and the result assigned to A)

SUBTRACTION

Matrices can be subtracted. Example:

160 MAT D = E - F

(F is subtracted from E and the result assigned to D)

MULTIPLICATION

Matrices can be multiplied. Example:

185 MAT G = H * J

(H is multiplied by J and the result is assigned to G)

INVERT

The named matrix is inverted. Example:

300 MAT K = INV (L)

(L is inverted and the result assigned to K)

TRANSPOSE

The named matrix is transposed. Example:

$$350 \ \text{MAT} \ M = \text{TRN} \ (N)$$

(N is transposed and the result assigned to M)

MULTIPLY BY CONSTANT

The named matrix is multiplied by a constant. That constant, which may be an algebraic expression is shown within parentheses. Example:

```
375 MAT S = (2) * T
380 MAT V = (K3) * T
385 MAT W = ((K3 * 2) + 6) * T
```

(T is multiplied by 2, the value of K3 and the value of (K3 * 2) + 6 respectively)

ZERO

The named matrix is filled out with zeros. In the example below that matrix is U:

$$450 \ \text{MAT} \ U = \text{ZER} \ (3, \ 4)$$

(The dimensions of U are defined as 4 x 5)

CONSTANT ONE

The named matrix is filled out with 1's. In the example below that matrix is V.

$$460 \ \text{MAT} \ V = \text{CØN} \ (I, \ J)$$

(The dimensions of V are defined as (I + 1) x (J + 1).)

IDENTITY

The named matrix is set up as an identity matrix. In the example below that matrix is W:

$$525 \text{ MAT } W = \text{IDN } (N, N)$$

(The dimensions of W are set up as $(N + 1)$ x $(N + 1)$.)

A matrix must be dimensioned. The DIM statement can, of course, be used. If no DIM statement is shown, the computer assigns "DIM n (10,10)" to the matrix, where n is its name. There are four MAT statements which can redefine matrix sizes while the program is in execution. They are READ, ZER, CON and IDN. The explanation of MAT READ above is a good illustration of how redefining can be done.

Once the exact dimensions of a matrix have been defined, the computer remembers them for the duration of the BASIC program, or until the dimensions are changed.

Matrix computations can also involve column and row vectors. A column vector is defined as a single-subscripted array; a row vector is defined as a double-subscripted array where the first part of the subscript is zero. Here's an example:

$$625 \text{ DIM } P(5), Q(0, 5)$$

(P can be used as a 6-element column vector and Q as a 6-element row vector.)

The same matrix name may appear on both sides of the equals sign in a BASIC statement but only one operation can be shown on the right-hand side of the equals sign. This statement is illegal:

$$825 \text{ MAT } C = A + B + C$$

But these statements are OK:

825 MAT C = B + C
830 MAT C = A + C

The way to make one matrix exactly equal another is shown by this statement:

900 MAT X = (1) * Y

This would be equivalent to writing:

900 MAT X = Y

if that form existed. It does not and the computer will give an error message if you should try to use it.

EXERCISE

Tell what's wrong with these matrix instructions. Consider them as independent examples:

150 READ X(3, 4)
180 MAT READ X1(3, 2)
200 MAT R = CØNSTANT
210 MAT X = Y
225 MAT G = H - P + Q
250 MAT T = 3 * T

Lesson 16

HOME-MADE FUNCTIONS

You saw in an earlier lesson that there are a number of functions built right into the BASIC language. Some examples are SIN, COS, SQR.

If you need the square root of $(I+Q)/R$ all you have to do is call for the execution of the SQR function like this:

$$15 \text{ LET } V3 = \text{SQR} ((I+Q)/R)$$

The computer will first calculate $(I+Q)/R$, then compute its square root, and finally assign the result to V3.

Similarly, when you need the sine, cosine, log, etc., of some value, you place that value within parentheses following the name of the appropriate function. The value, which may be a complicated expression, is called the "argument" of the function. Here are examples showing how arguments may be written:

```
200 LET  P = SIN(R) + CØS(J)
210 LET  S = LØG (10)
220 LET  W = EXP (C ↑ 2 - D ↑ 2)
230 LET  Z = INT (F + .5)
```

The complete list of BASIC functions was shown in an earlier lesson.

Suppose the list of BASIC functions does not include some function you need. You need not be dismayed. Build your own! Here's how a function is defined.

First decide upon a 3-letter name for your function. The first two letters must be FN. Then show one argument in parentheses. Finally show how that argument is to be used by writing a statement which begins with DEF (DEF means "define").

An example will help make this clear. Suppose you need a function which converts degrees to radians. The mathematical constant by which degrees have to be multiplied in order to get radians, is 3.14159265/180.

The function would be:

$$60 \ \ DEF \ \ FNC(D) = D \ * \ (3.14159265/180)$$

Study the function to see how it's been constructed. The decision to call it FNC is your choice, but of course the letters FN are required as the first two letters.

The argument D appears both at the left and to the right of the equals sign. At the left is shown the name of the function's argument, and at the right, how the argument is used. Only one argument may be shown in a function's definition but extended BASIC permits more. See Lesson 24.

Don't subscript the argument name in a function's definition. Don't use that argument name any place else in your program. It's a "dummy" name. When the function you've defined is actually used in your program, actual arguments are given. This last sentence may sound a bit puzzling, but look at this example:

Lesson 16

```
10 READ R

20 DEF FNC(D) = (D * 3.14159265/180)

30 LET Q = FNC(R)

40 PRINT Q

50 READ T

60 LET W = FNC(T) + FNC (T ↑ 2)

70 PRINT W

80 DATA 62.6, 98.7

99999 END
```

Figure 16-1

At line number 20 the FNC function is defined. The "dummy" argument is D. When the function is used, it is first used with the actual argument R, then later with actual arguments T and T ↑ 2.

Those actual arguments are treated the same way that D is treated in the function's definition. The function definition, therefore, acts as a model to show how actual arguments are to be handled.

In other words, when FNC is called for at line number 30, the computer will multiply R by 3.1415926/180 and assign the result to Q. At line number 60, the computer will multiply T by 3.14159265/180, save the result, then multiply T ↑ 2 (T squared) by 3.14159265/180 and add that result to the saved result. The sum will be assigned to W.

A "home-made" function can be defined any place in your program, before or after it is actually used. That definition can include the standard BASIC functions, EXP, INT, SQR, etc., but it cannot include any home-made functions.

A function can use values calculated <u>earlier</u> in the program. For instance, suppose we need a function which <u>gives</u> the square root of $a^2 + b^2$:

```
10 DEF FNS(X) = SQR (X ↑ 2 + B ↑ 2)

20 LET B = 10

20 READ A

40 LET Y = FNS (A)

50 PRINT Y

60 GØ TØ 30

70 DATA 5, 10, 15, 20, 25

99999 END
```

Figure 16-2

In this illustration B has the constant value 10. Its name is shown in the <u>definition</u> of the function FNS. We can see it is not the <u>variable</u> argument of the function; X is. Therefore, when the function is called for (see line number 40), the value of A replaces the variable X but the value of B is used as it was set earlier in the program.

Functions which are useful to engineers and mathematicians, but which are not included in the list of BASIC statements are sinh $x = 1/2 \ (e^x - e^{-x})$ and cosh $x = 1/2 \ (e^x + e^{-x})$. These are easily defined as:

```
10 DEF FNG(X) = (EXP(X) - EXP(-X))/2      (Hyperbolic sine)

20 DEF FNH(X) = (EXP(X) + EXP(-X))/2      (Hyperbolic cosine)
```

Of course, more than one function can be defined in a program; as many as 26 can be defined, in fact. However, those definitions are good for the current program only. If another program requires the same functions, they must be defined in that program too.

Some discretion should be exercised when defining functions. There's no point defining a function which is going to be used only once in a program. The reason is obvious; one may just as well show the function he needs as an equation at the exact place in his program where he needs it, rather than go to all the trouble of defining that equation as a function.

EXERCISE

Define functions to correspond with these equations. Use function names FNY, FNP and FND respectively.

$$x^3 + x^2$$

$$r + 6$$

$$\sin j + \cos j$$

Show uses of these defined functions as they would appear in a BASIC program at line numbers 80, 85 and 90.

Lesson 17

SUBROUTINES

In the last lesson you saw that if an equation is to be used over and over again in your program, you can write a function to express the equation. Then, whenever the equation is needed, you can name the function and automatically get the results wanted.

In BASIC the same idea can be used where portions of your program are concerned. Suppose you need the same half dozen or so statements in your program over and over again. There's no necessity to write those statements over and over. You can write them once and have the computer branch to them whenever they're needed.

Here's the outline of a BASIC program which illustrates this principle:

```
100 READ A, B, C

200 GØSUB 2000

300 PRINT X

        .
        .
        .
        .
800 LET A = J * Q

810 LET B = P - L

820 LET C = (W + X) * Z

830 GØSUB 2000

840 PRINT X
```

Dotted lines indicate statements not shown.

Figure 17-1 (Continued on next page)

```
        .
        .
        .
1200  LET  A = 49

1210  LET  B = SQR (46 + W)

1220  LET  C = 12.6

1230  GØSUB  2000

1240  PRINT  X

        .
        .
        .
2000  LET  K = (A * B) -C

2010  IF  K > 1500  THEN  2040

2020  LET  X = 0

2030  GØ TØ  2050

2040  LET  X = 1

2050  RETURN

        .
        .
        .
3000  DATA  40, 30, 25

99999 END
```

Figure 17-1 (Continued)

The statements at line numbers 2000 through 2050 constitute a "sub-routine." There may be as many statements as you need in a subroutine and the subroutine can be located anywhere in your program.

The GOSUB statements at line numbers 200, 830, and 1230 act almost like "GO TO" statements. They cause the computer to branch to the statement at line number 2000. There's a difference, though. The computer remembers where it was when it jumps to the statement at line number 2000. When the computer encounters the RETURN statement in the subroutine, it goes back to the statement immediately following the GOSUB statement which it executed last.

You can see that every subroutine must have at least one RETURN statement. These RETURN statements cause the computer to branch back to the main parts of the program after the subroutines called have been executed.

You can have several subroutines in your BASIC program if you need them. Each subroutine is called by GOSUB statements. Be careful not to let the computer fall inadvertently into a subroutine without having been sent there by a GOSUB statement. The RETURN statement when executed will cause all kinds of confusion for the computer.

It's perfectly all right though to have the computer branch completely around a subroutine using an ordinary GO TO statement. This will allow you to place subroutines anywhere you please in a program. Cautious people place their subroutines at the end of their programs.

Subroutines may call other subroutines. That is, subroutines may be "nested." Nesting can be carried out to any desired depth. You must remember, though, that the RETURN statement in a subroutine will cause the program to return to the statement immediately following the GOSUB statement which the computer executed last.

EXERCISE

Write a subroutine to calculate P from values of X, Y and Z. If the value of P computed is less than 6, have the computer stop; if the value is equal to 6, have the computer add 3 to the value of P; then have it return to the main program. If the value of P is greater than 6, have the computer return at once to the main program.

Lesson 18

THE INPUT STATEMENT

In earlier lessons we showed two ways to tell the computer about numbers to be used in programs. One way is to write down some name, then give it a value. Therefore,

        20 LET X 1 = 6
        30 LET L = 21.7
        40 LET P = 14.6E3

are all legal ways to tell the computer about numbers. The names X1, L and P, in this example, will hold the values shown throughout the duration of the program, or until those values are changed by the program. You've seen examples of how the value assigned to a name can be changed:

        50 LET K = K + 1

Here, there are two values for K, an old one and a new one. The old value of K is used in a calculation. The value 1 is added to the old K value. The result of the calculation becomes the new value of K. At that moment the old value of K disappears.

The value for K is stored at a definite location in the computer's memory. That location can hold only one number. That's why when a new value is created, the old one, having the same name, is lost.

Another way to tell the computer about numbers is by use of the DATA statement. The DATA statement looks like this:

        20 DATA 1.2, 7.4, 6, 8.9, -2, -4.7, 6.23E4

Whenever the computer executes a READ statement, the computer picks up one or more of the values in the DATA statement. The computer remembers which value it took last from that statement. This means that if the computer keeps executing one or more READ statements, values are taken from the DATA statement in sequential order. When the last value has been taken from the DATA statement, the computer will stop. The computer will type a message saying it's "out of data."

You may place as many DATA statements in your program as you need. They can be sprinkled any place in your program. The computer will use the values in those statements in the same order that the DATA statements have been written.

Ordinarily when a value has been taken from a DATA statement, that value cannot be used again. However, the RESTORE statement will cause the computer to begin reading values again from the beginning of the DATA statement. Here's an example:

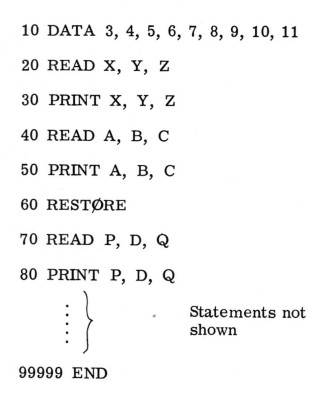

```
10 DATA 3, 4, 5, 6, 7, 8, 9, 10, 11

20 READ X, Y, Z

30 PRINT X, Y, Z

40 READ A, B, C

50 PRINT A, B, C

60 RESTØRE

70 READ P, D, Q

80 PRINT P, D, Q
       .
       .          Statements not
       .          shown
       .

99999 END
```

Figure 18-1

The values assigned to X, Y, and Z are 3, 4, and 5 respectively; those assigned to A, B, and C are 6, 7, and 8.

The values assigned to P, D, and Q are 3, 4 and 5 respectively. If the RESTORE statement had not been written at line number 60, the computer would have assigned values 9, 10, and 11 to P, D, and Q.

A third way of telling the computer about numbers is by use of the IN-PUT statement. That statement looks like this:

160 INPUT V

When the computer executes the statement at line number 160, it will type a question mark (?) on the teletypewriter paper at the left-hand side of a new line; then the computer will wait.

It will be the computer user's responsibility to type in a value following that question mark. That value will be assigned to the name, or names, shown in the INPUT statement.

In this example, suppose the computer user types a number such as 20.3. That value will be assigned to V.

Then the computer will continue the program with the statement which follows the INPUT statement. Let's look at an example program:

```
10 INPUT I, J, K

20 PRINT I * J * K

30 GØ TØ 10

99999 END
```

Figure 18-2

This is a complete program which will run as long as the computer user wants it to run. When the computer types a question mark on a fresh line of the teletypewriter's paper, the computer user must type in three numbers. Those numbers will be used in the program beginning immediately following the location of the INPUT statement. In this simple example, the three numbers will be multiplied together, and the product will be printed out.

Then the computer will branch back to statement 10, and the procedure will be repeated.

The computer user must type the three numbers separated by commas. If he does this incorrectly, or if he types in either less than, or more than three numbers, the computer will tell him he made a mistake and will ask him to try again.

Of course the computer user must be familiar enough with his program so that he knows how many numbers to type in when he gets the signal (a question mark typed at the beginning of a line).

One way to make a program more clear is to have the computer print a message before the question mark is typed. This is easily done:

```
10  PRINT ''ENTER  RADIUS  VALUE''

20  INPUT  R

30  PRINT  3.1416 * R * R, R

40  GØ TØ 10

99999  END
```

Figure 18-3

Before the computer types the question mark, it will type out ENTER RADIUS VALUE. Now the user will know how many values he has to type (in this case, one) and what the use of that value is in the program.

This illustrative program, of course, calculates the areas of circles and prints out both the calculated areas and the corresponding radius values.

Lesson 18

The INPUT statement is a very useful statement, but it should be used with some discretion. Its use is not as efficient as the READ and DATA statement combinations. You may find that it'll slow down the operation of your program.

EXERCISE

Write a program where values of principal and interest rate are to be read into the computer using the INPUT statement. Have the computer compute interest by multiplying interest rate times principal; then have the computer print out the interest cost.

Have the computer branch back to evaluate other interest costs.

Have the computer type out a message telling the computer user what to type in after the question mark appears.

Lesson 19

LIBRARY

We saw in earlier lessons that a computer user may save a program at the computer site. In order to recall that program another day, all the user needs to remember is the name he gave that program.

There's no chance that a user's program will get confused with another program someone else wrote and to which he gave the same name. Programs are kept segregated by user numbers. The programs which a user has saved become part of his personal library. If he ever wants to know how many programs are in this library, and what the program names are, the user can type at any time:

CATALØG

The computer will type out all the programs which are currently saved in the user's library.

If the user also wants to know how large each program is, he can type CASALOG instead of CATALOG. This way:

CASALØG

The computer will list each program in the user's library and type a "size" in characters. The maximum size which programs may have is about 6200 characters. Later you'll see how a user can keep checking the size of his program as he writes it.

A user ordinarily cannot access a program in a personal library other than his own. This is a useful protective device though it has some disadvantages. Lesson 22 has a comment about how a limited amount of program sharing is possible.

There is a library available in "time-sharing" which is accessible by all users. This library includes in it a number of programs which are useful and/or educational.

All a user needs to know are the names of these programs and he can call for them at any time. Here is how a user can get a list of time-sharing library programs. The user types:

ØLD

The computer inquires what "OLD" program the user wants, to which he replies CATLOG***. Note the three asterisks. They're necessary. Study this conversation:

ØLD
ØLD PRØBLEM NAME -- CATLØG***
READY
LIST

When the user types LIST, the computer types out a guide to all the system's library programs.

A time-sharing installation will supply, upon request, a little booklet containing library programs. The information given therein gives the names of the programs, what they do, how to use them, and samples of their use.

Programs available are of two kinds, those which provide practical useful results and those which are used for demonstrations. The useful ones can be used for doing statistical analyses, fitting curves, solvings sets of linear equations, finding roots, and others; the demonstration programs can be used to play "Black Jack" with the computer, play TIC TAC TOE, take math examinations, and others. Some programs plot answers as well as write them out.

The way to call for one of these system library programs is to go through the "OLD" sequence, and give the program's name. Note the three asterisks in the program's name. They are always needed:

ØLD
ØLD PRØBLEM NAME -- SAVING***
READY

The program will be ready for execution. In general, when a program is called, the user must type RUN. The computer will give whatever instructions are required to run the program. Let's talk about SAVING***.

SAVING*** is a library program which calculates the amount of money that would accumulate after N years at an annual interest rate R compounded T times per year, when the initial amount is P and an amount D is added at the beginning of each subsequent year.

When we type the word RUN, the following instructions will be typed out:

SAVING

THIS PRØGRAM CALCULATES THE AMØUNT ØF MØNEY THAT WØULD ACCUMULATE AFTER N YEARS AT AN ANNUAL INTEREST RATE R CØMPØUNDED T TIMES PER YEAR, WHEN THE INITIAL AMØUNT IS P AND AN AMØUNT D IS ADDED AT THE BEGINNING ØF EACH SUB-SEQUENT YEAR. NØTE THAT P AND D ARE GIVEN IN DØLLARS, N AND T MUST BE INTEGERS, AND R IS GIVEN AS A PERCENTAGE.

WHAT ARE P, D, N, T, R

?

At this point the user types in the values requested and the computer gives the desired information.

The computer will then ask whether you have another case you want to try. If so, you give the information it wants, or you stop the program by telling it "no."

Here is a short list of system library programs which are representative of about 50 BASIC programs available at the time of this writing. The user should get an up-to-date listing either by getting the library manual mentioned earlier, or by listing the special informative program CATLOG***:

TRUINT*** Calculates the true annual interest rate charged on an installment loan.

CØLINR*** Computes confidence limits on simple linear regressions.

ZERØES*** Locates the values of X at which relative maximums and minimums of F (X) occur, and the values of X for which F (X) is zero.

SIMEQN***   Solves systems consisting of N linear equations in N unknowns.

RØØTER***   Finds the roots of polynomials using Bairstow's method.

BITEST***   Makes a statistical test of a binomial proportion.

PLØTTØ***   Plots 1 to 6 functions of X simultaneously.

TWØPLØ***   Plots 2 functions of a variable X simultaneously.

CURFIT***   Determines which of 6 curves best fits the supplied data.

TICTAC***   Plays TIC TAC TOE with you.

BLKJAK***   Plays Black Jack with you.

EXERCISE

Assume you're contemplating taking out a loan at your friendly neighborhood bank for the purpose of buying a car, and you want to call the system library program which calculates true annual interest rate. Show your conversation with the computer beginning with the word OLD, and terminating with the word READY.

Lesson 20

PAPER TAPE USAGE

If your teletype machine has paper tape input/output capability, you may want to punch programs on paper tape before you call up the computer. Then, when the computer requests your program, you can read it in from tape. Reading tape is faster than typing, and you will therefore save time.

Another thing you may want to do is to save a program on paper tape rather than at the computer site. Doing this will save money since you must pay for storage when you save a program at the computer's location.

This lesson tells how you can punch and read in paper tape.

PUNCH OFF-LINE

First, let's punch a tape "off-line." By "off-line" we mean that we do this without being connected to the computer.

Sit at the teletype machine and push down the button marked LCL. You should hear the machine's motor come to life. Now follow these steps:

1. Depress paper tape punch ON button.

2. Hit space bar on key board about 20 times.

3. Return carriage by hitting RETURN key.

4. Hit RUBOUT key on keyboard about 20 times.

5. Type your program in. At the end of each line, hit the RETURN key and the LINE FEED key in that order.

6. When your program has been completely typed in, hit RUBOUT again about 20 times.

7. Depress paper tape punch OFF button.

If you should make a mistake while punching your tape, hit the RETURN and LINE FEED keys; then retype the entire line. Soon we'll show you alternate ways of making corrections.

Now write the name of your program at the beginning of the tape, and you're ready to read it into the computer.

READ TAPE

Call up the computer, give it your user number, tell it that you want to write a new program in BASIC.

When you've given the new program name, the computer types:

READY

You reply:

TAPE

The computer will again type:

READY

Now follow these steps:

1. Release the tape gate on the paper tape reader by pressing the lock button.

2. Place the tape surface facing upward with the feed holes over the tape feed wheel and position the tape so that the RUBOUT characters are over the sensing pins.

3. Close and lock the gate by pushing down.

4. Put the tape-read switch in the START position.

Lesson 20

5. The tape will read into the computer's memory. When reading has been completed, put the tape-read switch back in OFF position.

6. Type:

KEY

At the conclusion of Step 6, proceed with your program as if you'd typed it in manually.

PUNCH TAPE

Suppose you have just written a program you'd like to save on paper tape. Do this:

First type:

TAPE

The computer will type:

READY

Turn ON the paper tape punch unit as you did when you punched a tape "off-line"

Now do this:

1. Hit the space bar on the keyboard about 20 times.

2. Return the carriage by hitting RETURN.

3. Hit the RUBOUT key on the keyboard about 20 times.

4. Turn the paper tape punch unit OFF as you did when punching tape "off-line."

5. Type LISTNH but don't return the carriage (don't hit RETURN).

6. Turn the paper tape punch unit ON again.

7. Hit the RETURN key.

The computer will punch your program on paper tape. At the conclusion, do this:

8. Hit the RUBOUT key about 20 times.

9. Turn OFF the paper tape punch unit.

10. Type:

KEY

The computer responds:

READY

Now you may tear off the tape and write the program's name at its beginning. Then you may proceed to some other programming function.

If you have a Model 35 Teletype Unit, call for library program TUT10$*** and run it. The program will tell you step by step how to use tape on that unit.

Lesson 21

MAKING CORRECTIONS

If you should make a mistake while typing a line, you may return the carriage (by hitting the RETURN key) and correct the error by retyping the entire line.

If you prefer not to do this and the error involves only a few characters, you can use the character " ← " to make corrections. Each time you type ← , the computer in effect backspaces one character-position. You may "strike over" the error, thus correcting it. Here's an example:

$$50 \ LET \ P \ = \ R*S+T \leftarrow \ \leftarrow *T$$

In this example, the user had intended the expression to read R*S*T. Instead he wrote R*S+T. The two ←'s had the effect of repositioning the computer at the character position following "S." The characters *T then replaced +T.

Another way to make corrections is to hit the "ESC" key at any time you're typing a line. Doing this will cause the entire line to be disregarded. It will not be entered in your program.

Whenever you hit the "ESC" key, the computer will type 'DELETED" on the same line and return the carriage. Now, you can begin the line afresh.

You may use the system "EDIT" commands to make changes or corrections. Lesson 23 will show how this is done.

Incidentally, on Model 35 Teletype Units, the ESC key is labeled "ALT MODE."

Lesson 22

SYSTEM COMMANDS AND FEATURES

There are a number of commands you can give the remote computer which are not strictly part of the BASIC language. They're called "System Commands." You've seen some of these commands already. For example:

> LISTNH
> SAVE
> UNSAVE
> ØLD
> NEW
> RUN
> LIST

You used these words before. They tell the computer about things you want it to do. Those "things" are only indirectly connected with a program you may be writing. Note that system commands never begin with a line number. This is one infallible way you can distinguish between a BASIC command, such as PRINT or LET, and a system command such as LIST or RUN.

In this lesson we'll discuss the entire repertoire of system commands except the EDIT instructions, which we'll cover in the next lesson.

RUN

When you have written a program and you want the computer to execute it, type at the beginning of the next line:

> RUN

Then return the carriage (hit the RETURN key on the keyboard). The computer will run your program or tell you why it cannot.

If this command is given while your program is in execution, the computer will tell how long your program has been running so far.

Lesson 22

LIST

Whenever you want the computer to give you a complete listing of your program, including all changes you've made to the moment, type:

LIST

The computer will give a brief heading, then list your program from the beginning. If you don't want a complete listing, type:

LIST--40

The computer will begin listing your program at line number 40. Of course any desired line number can be written instead of 40.

The command:

LISTNH

will list your entire program without a heading.

The command:

LISTNH250

will list your program without a heading beginning at line number 250. You may show any desired line number, of course.

Observe the difference between **LIST--40** and **LISTNH250**. Follow the model examples exactly.

SAVE

This command will cause the computer to save the program you're working on. You can still change or add to the program even though it's been saved. When typing in a large program, it's a good idea to type:

SAVE

periodically to protect yourself against computer malfunctions. (They do occur, though infrequently.)

OLD

If you need to access a saved program, type:

ØLD

The computer will ask for its name. Give the name and the computer will make the saved program available to you.

UNSAVE

If you should want to unsave a program you saved earlier, call for it, then type UNSAVE.

NEW

At any time you want to begin writing a new program, type:

NEW

The computer will ask for its name. When you have given it, the computer will give you the "go ahead" by typing:

READY

SCRATCH

Suppose you want to wipe out all the instructions of some program you're working on. Type:

SCRATCH

All statements will be wiped out. The name of the program, as you gave it earlier, will be unchanged. Whatever new statements you write will be assigned to the program.

RENAME

You may rename a program you're working on at any time. Simply type:

RENAME

The computer will ask for a new name. This command can be used to save system library programs in your own library. Do it this way:

```
ØLD
ØLD  PRØBLEM  NAME -- ØNEWAY***
READY
RENAME
NEW  PRØBLEM  NAME -- MYPRØG
READY
```

The library program ONEWAY*** will be available in your library under your name MYPROG (or whatever else you wish to call it).

LENGTH

Type this system command when you need to know about how many characters are in use in the program you're currently working on. BASIC programs are limited in length and it's helpful to know how close you are to the maximum. At the time of this writing, a program may employ up to 6200 characters. This figure should be taken with some caution because table sizes, as defined by DIM statements, should be taken into consideration.

It's likely that the maximum sizes of programs you write, will be liberalized. You may have to do some independent research on this point.

HELLO

This command should be used when another user is ready to take over after you have finished your work but have not typed GOODBYE.

The new user simply types:

```
HELLØ
```

The computer inquires about the new user's number, the language to be used, etc.

SYSTEM

The word SYSTEM is typed when a user wants to change from one programming language to another. (FORTRAN and ALGOL are available on the system as well as BASIC.) The computer will inquire what new language you want to use.

When you call for a library program, you should be sure that the language mode you're in, matches the language that the library program is written in. If it doesn't match, you'll get many error messages when you ask that the program be run. If this happens, change the system language to match the program and try again.

STATUS

Type the word STATUS if you want to know whether the computer is idle or running a program for you at any given moment.

STOP

Type the word STOP when you want the computer to cease what it's doing for you. Often, the letter "S" will work just as well. Don't forget to return the carriage (to hit the RETURN key) whenever you type "S" or STOP. Another way to stop the computer is to hold down the CONTROL and SHIFT keys simultaneously and hit "P" at the same time. We recommend the latter method.

BYE or GOODBYE

Type the word BYE or GOODBYE when you want to be disconnected from the computer.

CATALOG or CASALOG

Type the word CATALOG or CASALOG when you want to know what programs are saved under your user number. CATALOG simply lists them; CASALOG also gives their length in characters.

There's a difference between requesting a list of programs under your user number versus a list of what's in the system library. When you need the former, type the word CATALOG or CASALOG at the beginning of a new line; when you need the latter type:

ØLD

Then, when the computer requests the "old program name," type CATLØG***.

The computer will type:

READY

You type:

LIST

and you'll get a complete guide to all system library programs.

TTY

Type TTY and the computer will tell you what number teletype you're connected to and a few other things about your connection, such as your user number and what program you're working on.

TAPE and KEY

These two system commands are associated with tape usage. Review the tape usage lesson.

ABBREVIATIONS

When you need to type a system command, you may simply type the first three letters. Thus, CAT for CATALOG, SAV for SAVE, SCR for SCRATCH, etc. will suffice.

PROGRAM PROTECTION

When you invent a name for an important program, use a dollar sign ($) as the sixth character. When you save the program, no one will ever be able to list it (not even you). Example names you can use are: TEST-$, SAMPL$, ALPHA$. These programs can be retrieved from your library and even changed, but they can't be listed, renamed or punched out on paper tape.

If the sixth character of your program name is an asterisk (*), the program can be made available to several users under different user numbers. See your sales representative about this feature if it sounds like something you can use.

Lesson 23

EDIT COMMANDS

There are 5 EDIT commands. Their names and a brief idea of what they do is shown below:

EDIT DELETE   —   Deletes portions of the program you're working on.

EDIT EXTRACT   —   Retains portions of the program you're working on.

EDIT MERGE   —   Combines saved programs into a temporary working area, and resequences line numbers.

EDIT WEAVE   —   Combines saved programs into a temporary working area, but does not resequence line numbers.

EDIT RESEQUENCE —   Resequences line numbers of the programs, you're working on.

EDIT DELETE

Suppose you are working on a program and wish to delete portions of it. You may type:

EDIT DELETE 25,50-100,500-99999,10

This command will cause the statements at line numbers 25 and 10 to be wiped out. Also statements from 50 to 100 (inclusive) will be wiped out. Further, statements from 500 thru 99999 will be deleted. When you write "99999," it's the same as saying "to the end of the program."

It doesn't matter if some of the line numbers you've mentioned don't exist. The computer will assume they do, and wipe them out. For instance if you type:

EDIT DELETE 50-100

and your program includes statements at only line numbers 60 and 70, then those statements will be deleted.

Don't overlap when you write the EDIT DELETE command. This next command is illegal:

EDIT DELETE 100-200,150,160-300

Line number 150 is illegally included, as is 160-300. The intent of this command could be communicated by writing:

EDIT DELETE 100-300

EDIT EXTRACT

EDIT EXTRACT is the complement of EDIT DELETE. The command retains what you reference, and deletes everything else. For example:

EDIT EXTRACT 100-200,99999

This command will retain only the statements at line numbers 100 thru 200 and 99999 in the program you're working on. Everything else will be eliminated.

EDIT RESEQUENCE

This command permits you to renumber the lines of the program you're working on. There are a number of ways to use it. Here's one:

EDIT RESEQUENCE

The computer will resequence your program beginning with line number 100, and increment line numbers by 10.

Here's another way:

EDIT RESEQUENCE 200,30,20

The computer will resequence your program beginning with line 30 of your program (leaving lines 0 thru 29 untouched). The new line numbers will begin with line number 200 and lines will be incremented by 20.

The general form of EDIT RESEQUENCE is:

EDIT RESEQUENCE N,L,I

where: N = new line number to be assigned to the program line where re-sequencing is to begin.

L = old line number in the program where resequencing is to begin.

I = increment value between line numbers.

L may be zero. If I is not given, the computer assumes you want the increment to be 10. If N is not specified, the computer assumes you want to begin resequencing with line number 100.

In BASIC programs, whenever resequencing is requested, all internal line number references are adjusted so that your program works as well as it did before resequencing was performed.

EDIT MERGE

With this command, you can combine two or more saved programs into one program which is placed in your temporary working area. Here's an example:

EDIT MERGE ALPHA,BETA

The two programs will be combined and resequenced beginning with statement number 100. The increment between statement numbers will be 10. The complete program BETA will follow the complete program ALPHA. If both programs have END statements, both will be included in the new program.

The new program will now be available to you as if you had just typed it yourself. You can now change, modify or delete statements.

An important point to observe is that before EDIT MERGE can be utilized, you must have some program in your working area. It can be either of the programs involved in the MERGE command or an entirely different program. In the latter case, the program disappears when MERGE is executed. Only the programs named in the MERGE command remain in your working area. The name of the working area is the name it had before MERGE was called for.

The general form for EDIT MERGE is:

EDIT MERGE M,F1,L1,......... FN,LN

where: M is the main program and F1, F2 ..... FN are subsidiary programs which are merged or appended to it. L1, L2 ...... LN are optional line numbers telling where in the main program the subsidiary programs are to be placed. Those subsidiary programs are placed following the line numbers given in the MERGE command.

Up to 9 programs may be named in the EDIT MERGE command.

EDIT WEAVE

This command is very similar to EDIT MERGE. One difference is that resequencing is not done after two or more programs have been joined.

Another difference is that where involved programs have common line numbers, only the line number of the last program listed in the command will be kept.

An example of EDIT WEAVE is this:

EDIT WEAVE WIN,PLACE,SHØW

The three programs will be joined in consecutive order, but where line numbers are common in WIN, PLACE and SHOW, those appearing in SHOW will over-ride WIN and PLACE. Where line numbers are common in WIN and PLACE, those appearing in PLACE will over-ride WIN.

Up to 9 programs may be named in the EDIT WEAVE command.

EDIT

If you should need a brief sketch of how the EDIT commands work, type EDIT and return the carriage. The computer will give further instructions telling how to proceed.

EDIT commands are being improved. We'd suggest that you do some independent research to see what their latest implementation is.

Lesson 24

BASIC is a dynamic language and is constantly being improved. At the time of this writing several new features are planned. They may be available on your computer now. This lesson discusses the new features planned. Check to see if you have them.

ALPHA MANIPULATION

BASIC will be able to handle, not only numeric information, but also alphabetic or alphanumeric (digits, letters, and other characters) information.

Here are some of the things you will be able to do:

```
10 LET A$ = " END"

20 LET B$ = "THE"

30 PRINT B$; A$

99999 END
```

Figure 24-1

Note the quotation marks around the values END and THE. They are required. When this program is executed, the computer will print:

THE END

beginning at the left-hand side of the teletype paper. Note the use of semicolons. Commas will work but the words THE and END will be spread out more.

Note the dollar signs ($) following variable names A and B. These tell the computer that the alpha mode is required. The rules for forming variable names are otherwise unchanged. Simply append the dollar signs.

Alpha information can be read from DATA statements:

```
10  READ X5$

20  PRINT X5$

30  DATA THIS IS A SAMPLE PRØGRAM

99999  END
```

Figure 24-2

When the program is executed, the message

THIS IS A SAMPLE PRØGRAM

will be printed out.

Sometimes you'll have to place quotation marks around alpha information. Do so if the item begins with a digit or if it has an imbedded comma. Here's an example:

```
10  READ X$, Y$, Z$

20  PRINT X$; Y$; Z$

30  DATA DATE IS , "5 JULY, ", "1969"

99999  END
```

Figure 24-3

The three data values, separated by commas, are:

DATE IS
5 JULY,
1969

When the program is executed, the computer will print out:

DATE IS 5 JULY, 1969

You may use alpha information in combination with the INPUT statement and with IF statements. The rules for using quotation marks for INPUT statements are the same as for DATA statements. The rules for using quotation marks for IF statements are the same as for LET statements. If in doubt about quotation marks, put them in. Superfluous quotation marks will be ignored.

These statements are OK:

IF P$ > "END" THEN 450

IF Q$ = "BASIC" THEN 200

IF R$(J+1) < = R$(K) THEN 260

A few notes of interest are these:

1. DIM statements can be written for alpha arrays. Alpha arrays can be subscripted.

2. The relational symbol > means "later in alphabetic order." The symbols < and = have similar meanings. When comparing alpha items, trailing blanks are ignored. Thus, "END" and "END " are "equal." Digits are "smaller" than letters; so are most symbols. You'll have to do some experimenting if you want to get into making unusual comparisons.

3. Alpha symbols in data items are known as "strings." A string may contain up to 60 characters.

4. Numeric and string data are kept in separate blocks; they act independently of each other. The command RESTØRE will restore only the numerical data. To restore string data, use RESTØRE$.

Lesson 24

RANDOMIZE

A new feature uses the word RANDOM or RANDOMIZE. Place this instruction at the beginning of a program which calls for the RND (random number) instruction. Every time you run the program you'll get a different set of random numbers. Example:

```
10 RANDØM

20 FØR K = 1 TØ 50

30 LET P=RND(X)

40 PRINT P;

50 NEXT K

99999 END
```

Figure 24-4

This program will give 50 different random numbers each time that it's run.

LET

The LET statement will be liberalized. You'll be able to write statements like this:

$$25 \text{ LET } X = Y = Z(3) = 4.7*Q$$

X, Y and Z(3) will be assigned the value resulting from the calculation of 4.7 times Q. Use some common sense when you use this feature and you can't go wrong. Don't try "LET X = 3 = Y = Z," for example.

ON

A new BASIC statement permits multiple switching. The statement looks like this:

50 ØN P GØ TØ 30, 145, 200, 200, 90

When the computer executes this statement, it will branch to line numbers 30, 145, 200 or 90 depending upon what integer value P has. If P is 1, the computer branches to line number 30; if 2, to line number 145; if 3, to line number 200; if 4, to line number 200; and if 5 to line number 90.

P is set earlier in the program as a result of calculations or from a value read in from a DATA statement.

Any number of line numbers may follow GØ TØ. Some may repeat as shown in the example.

Any formula may be shown in place of P. The largest integer in the result is used to determine where the computer must branch.

If the calculation gives zero, a negative number or a number which is too large, an error condition will result.

IF

The extended version of BASIC permits either of these two ways of writing an IF statement:

30 IF X > Y THEN 46

or

30 IF X > Y GØ TØ 46

TAB

When you write PRINT statements you'll be able to tabulate the teletypewriter. Positions on the paper are assumed numbered from zero to 74. Here's how it is done:

430 PRINT A; TAB (15); B; TAB (25); C

The value of A will be printed beginning at column zero. The value of B will begin at column 15 and the value of C will begin at column 25.

DEF

The DEF statement is liberalized so that you may include more than one argument in the definition of a function. This definition is acceptable, for instance:

$$145 \quad DEF\ FNW(X, Y, Z) = SQR\ (X \uparrow 2 + Y \uparrow 2 + Z \uparrow 2)$$

MATRIX CHANGES AND EXTENSIONS

All matrices will use subscripts beginning with 1 instead of zero. This point is particularly important since it is a radical change from an earlier implementation. If you write:

$$35 \quad DIM\ A(20),\ B(5,6),\ C(3,1),\ D(1,3)$$

the A array (table) has 20 elements and the B array has 30 elements (5 rows and 6 columns).

C is a column vector and D is a row vector. Column vectors are always set up as nx1 matrices and row vectors are always set up as 1xn matrices.

DETERMINANTS

A variable called DET can be used in connection with the MAT INV command. After execution of the inversion, DET will equal the determinant of the inverted matrix. You can then decide whether the determinant is large enough for the inverse to be meaningful. Attempting to invert a singular matrix will set DET equal to zero. Here's a short program showing DET in use:

```
10 DIM X(5, 5)
20 MAT READ X
30 MAT B = INV (X)
40 PRINT "DETERMINANT IS " DET
50 MAT PRINT B
60 DATA 4, 6, 8, 2, 4, 3, 1, 8, 7, 4, 9, 5, 4, 3, 1, 2, 6, 7, 8, 9, 6, 5, 4, 3, 6
99999 END
```

Figure 24-5

MAT INPUT

The MAT INPUT command permits you to enter information into arrays, via teletypewriter while the program is in execution. At the same time, the variable NUM counts the number of values entered. NUM can be used for calculations or for any purpose ordinarily legal for other variables.

Here's an example of its use:

```
100 DIM X (50)

110 LET S = 0

120 MAT INPUT X

125 IF NUM = 0 GØ TØ 500

130 LET K = NUM

140 FØR I = 1 TØ K

150 LET S = S + X(I)

160 NEXT I

170 PRINT S,NUM

180 GØ TØ 110

500 PRINT "END ØF PRØGRAM"

99999 END
```

Figure 24-6

This program sums the values entered into the X array. Note the test at line number 125. When the carriage is returned with no value being entered, the computer will jump to the statement at line number 500.

Lesson 24

PASSWORDS

Extended BASIC permits you to save your program against unauthorized use. Type:

SAVE,JIMMY

and your program cannot be retrieved by anyone who doesn't know the password, JIMMY. The password you select can be any word which is written according to the rules for inventing program names. Don't forget it, though; you won't be able to retrieve your own program if you do.

Here's how you call for a program saved with a password.

ØLD

ØLD PRØBLEM NAME -- MYPRØG,JIMMY

READY

If you forget to give the password, the computer will ask for it.

When you save a program, you don't have to use passwords, of course. This is an optional feature.

Incidentally, we've taken some poetic license with the sequence shown above. In Extended BASIC, the computer will probably refer to programs as "files."

Lesson 25

A PROGRAM FROM BEGINNING TO END

In this lesson we show the sequence of events as a BASIC program was actually written, debugged, executed and saved.

Explanatory messages tell what's going on during each step. Underlined words were typed by the user. Not all user-typed lines are underlined, but you'll be able to see which they are from the appended remarks.

TIP 3 5 5

ØN AT 14:25   S1 MØN 08/07/67   TTY   5

USER NUMBER--S16448
SYSTEM--BAS
NEW ØR ØLD--NEW
NEW PRØBLEM NAME--SINCØS
READY.

CALLING
SEQUENCE

```
10 PRINT ''THIS PRØGRAM LISTS RADIAN VALUES AND CØRRESPØNDING''
20 PRINT ''SIN AND CØS VALUES.''
30 PRINT
40 INPUT X, Y
35 PRINT ''ENTER BEGINNING RADIAN VALUE AND STEP SIZE''
50 LET R=X
60 PRINT ''      R            SIN           CØS''
70 PRINT
80 PRINT R, SIN (R), CØS (R)
90 LET R=R+Y
100 IF R > 2*3.14159265 THEN 200
110 GØ TØ 80
99999 END
RUN
WAIT.
```

USER TYPES
IN PROGRAM.
NOTE: LINE
35 WILL BE
SORTED BY
COMPUTER
AHEAD OF
LINE 40.

-142-

Lesson 25

SINCØS   14:28   S1 MØN   08/07/67

UNDEFINED NUMBER   200

TIME: 0 SECS.

ERROR MESSAGE GIVEN BY COMPUTER

200 PRINT "END ØF PRØGRAM2
RUN

CORRECTION

SINCØS   14:28   S1 MØN   08/07/67

INCØRRECT   FØRMAT   IN 200

TIME: 0 SECS.

ERROR MESSAGE GIVEN BY COMPUTER

200 PRINT "END ØF PRØGRAM"
RUN

CORRECTION

SINCØS   14:29   S1 MØN   08/07/67

THIS PRØGRAM LISTS RADIAN VALUES AND CØRRESPØNDING
SIN AND CØS VALUES.

ENTER BEGINNING RADIAN VALUE AND STEP SIZE
? 1,.5

R	SIN	CØS
1	.841471	.540302
1.5	.997495	7.07372 E-2
2	.909297	-.416147
2.5	.598472	-.801144
3	.14112	

PROGRAM RUNS

MANUALLY STOPPED

STØP.
READY.

Lesson 25

```
LISTNH
10 PRINT "THIS PRØGRAM LISTS RADIAN VALUES AND CØRRESPØNDING"
20 PRINT "SIN AND CØS VALUES."
30 PRINT
35 PRINT "ENTER BEGINNING RADIAN VALUE AND STEP SIZE"
40 INPUT X, Y
50 LET R=X
60 PRINT "      R        SIN        CØS"
70 PRINT
80 PRINT R, SIN (R), CØS (R)
90 LET R=R+Y
100 IF R > 2*3.14159265 THEN 200
110 GØ TØ 80
200 PRINT "END ØF PRØGRAM"
99999 END
```

LISTING GIVEN BY COMPUTER

```
37  PRINT
60  PRINT "  R     SIN      CØS"
RUN
```

IMPROVEMENTS

SINCØS   14:31   S1 MØN   08/07/67

THIS PRØGRAM LISTS RADIAN VALUES AND CØRRESPØNDING
SIN AND CØS VALUES.

ENTER BEGINNING RADIAN VALUE AND STEP SIZE

```
?  1, 1.5
   R              SIN              CØS
1              .841471          .540302
2.5            .598472          -.801144
4              -.756802         -.653644
5.5            -.70554          .70867
END ØF PRØGRAM

TIME:    2 SECS.
```

PROGRAM RUNS

```
55  PRINT
RUN
```

IMPROVEMENT

SINCØS   14:32   S1 MØN 08/07/67

THIS PRØGRAM LISTS RADIAN VALUES AND CØRRESPØNDING SIN AND CØS VALUES.

ENTER BEGINNING RADIAN VALUE AND STEP SIZE

? 1, 2

R	SIN	CØS
1	.841471	.540302
3	.14112	-.989992
5	-.958924	.283662

END ØF PRØGRAM

TIME: 2 SECS.

PROGRAM RUNS

60 PRINT   "   R   SIN   CØS2
RUN

IMPROVEMENT

SINCØS   14:33   S1 MØN 08/07/67

INCØRRECT FØRMAT   IN 60

TIME: 0 SECS.

ERROR MESSAGE GIVEN BY COMPUTER

60 PRINT   "   R   SIN   CØS"
RUN

CORRECTION

SINCØS   14:33   S1 MØN 08/07/67

THIS PRØGRAM LISTS RADIAN VALUES AND CØRRESPØNDING SIN AND CØS VALUES.

ENTER BEGINNING RADIAN VALUE AND STEP SIZE

? .001, .0001

Lesson 25

R	SIN	CØS
.001	.001	1.
.0011	.0011	.999999
.0012	.0012	.999999
.0013	.0013	.999999
.0014	.0014	.999999
.0015	.0015	.999999
.0016	.0016	.999999
.0017	.0017	.999999
.0018	.0018	.999998
.0019	.0019	.999998
.002	.002	.9VK

PROGRAM
RUNS

MANUALLY
STOPPED

RAN   3 SEC.

STØP.

READY.

EDIT RESEQUENCE

READY.

RESEQUENCING

LIST

SINCØS   14:35   S1 MØN   08/07/67

```
100 PRINT "THIS PRØGRAM LISTS RADIAN VALUES AND CØRRESPØNDING"
110 PRINT "SIN AND CØS VALUES."
120 PRINT
130 PRINT "ENTER BEGINNING RADIAN VALUE AND STEP SIZE"
140 PRINT
150 INPUT X, Y
160 LET R=X
170 PRINT
180 PRINT      "      R          SIN           CØS"
190 PRINT
200 PRINT R, SIN(R), CØS(R)
210 LET R=R+Y
220 IF R >  2*3.14159265 THEN 240
230 GØ TØ 200
240 PRINT "END ØF PRØGRAM"
250 END
```

LISTING
GIVEN BY
COMPUTER

SAVE

READY

SINCØS   14:57   S1 MØN   08/07/67

THIS PRØGRAM LISTS RADIAN VALUES AND CØRRESPØNDING SIN AND CØS VALUES.

ENTER BEGINNING RADIAN VALUE AND STEP SIZE

? .314159265, 3←.314159265

R	SIN	CØS
.314159	.309017	.951057
.628319	.587785	.809017
.942478	.809017	.587785
1.25664	.951057	.309017
1.5708	1.	5.82077 E-9
1.88496	.951057	-.309017
2.19911	.809017	-.587785
2.51327	.587785	-.809017
2.82743	.309017	-.951057
3.14159	1.16997 E-8	-1.
3.45575	-.309017	-.951057
3.76991	-.587785	-.809017
4.08407	-.809017	-.587785
4.39823	-.951057	-.309017
4.71239	-1.	-3.50992 E-8
5.02655	-.951057	.309017
5.34071	-.809017	.587785
5.65487	-.587785	.809017
5.96903	-.309017	.951057
6.28319	-6.43195 E-8	1.

FINAL TEST RUN

END ØF PRØGRAM

TIME: 2 SECS.

BYE

*** ØFF AT 14:59   S1 MØN   08/07/67.

SIGNING OFF

Appendix

SUMMARY OF BASIC COMMANDS

COMMAND	PAGE REFERENCE
LET $v = x$	2,137
READ $v_1, v_2, \ldots v_n$	30
READ $a_1, a_2, \ldots a_n$	134
PRINT "m"	2,20,60
PRINT $v_1, v_2, \ldots v_n$	2,20,60
PRINT $a_1, a_2, \ldots a_n$	138
STØP	23
GØ TØ l	17,52
GØSUB l	106
RETURN	107
INPUT $v_1, v_2, \ldots v_n$	109,136
END	2,17
REM m	63
RESTORE	110
RESTORE$	136
MAT READ $v_1, v_2, \ldots v_n$	94,96
MAT PRINT $v_1, v_2 \ldots v_n$	96
MAT INPUT v	140
RANDOM	137
RANDOMIZE	137
FØR $c = b$ TØ e STEP s	70
NEXT c	70
DATA $n_1, n_2, \ldots n_n$	30

APPENDIX (SUMMARY OF BASIC COMMANDS) Continued

COMMAND	PAGE REFERENCE
DATA "a_1", "a_2", ... "a_n"	135
DIM $v_1 (d_1, d_2)$, $v_2 (d_1, d_2)$, ... $v_n (d_1, d_2)$	83
DIM $v_1 (d)$, $v_2 (d)$, ... $v_n (d)$	65
IF o_1 r o_2 THEN l	17,50
IF o_1 r o_2 GO TO l	138
ØN o GØ TØ l_1, l_2, ... l_n	137
DEF FNf(q_1, q_2, ... q_n) = k	139
DEF FNf(q) = k	102

v = variable name   e = ending value   r = relation

x = expression   s = step size   f = function name

m = message   n = numeric value   q = function argument

l = line number   a = alpha value   k = function definition

c = counter   d = dimension value

b = beginning value   o = operand

Answers

Lesson 1

1. There are two line number 30's.
2. FINIS is wrong. Should be END.
3. The name PI is illegal.
4. D cannot be used at line number 35. It hasn't been given a value.
5. There is no line number for one statement.
6. The word LET is missing at line 15.

Lesson 2

Line 15; * missing before K.
Line 20; LET missing.
Line 25; Better to write LET N = Y ↑ 6.
Line 30; /* together are meaningless.
Line 35; Missing "open" parentheses.

Lesson 4

```
10 LET  B = 0
20 LET  D = 0
30 PRINT B*D
40 IF  B*D > 25000 THEN 99999
50 LET  B = B + 1
60 LET  D = D + 1
70 GØ TØ 30
99999 END
```

Lesson 5

```
10 READ R
20 PRINT 3.1416*R*R
30 GØ TØ 10
40 DATA 2.1, 1.3, 6, 4.8, 9.2, 4.1, 2.2, 1.8, .247, 63
99999 END
```

Answers to Selected Exercises

Lesson 6

1. Errors are:
   Line 30; * incorrectly used. Omit it.
   Line 40; A number must be shown ahead of E.
   Line 50; Too many digits in the number.
2. Possible answers are:
   -1.46E1
   .34E-3
   21.146E0

Lesson 7

Line 10; Parentheses incorrectly used.   Two names at left of equals.
Line 20; LET missing.
Line 30; Missing "close" parentheses.
Line 40; */ together are meaningless.
Line 50; = G incorrectly placed.
Line 60; ÷ should be /.
Line 70; No equals shown.
Line 80; Too many equals.
Line 90; Missing * indicating multiplication.
Line 100; ** meaningless in BASIC.

Lesson 9

```
10 READ V
20 IF V = 8.3 THEN 40
30 GØ TØ 10
40 LET X = V ↑ 3.
50 PRINT X
60 DATA 26.2, 15.7, 18.6, 8.3
99999 END
```

Lesson 12

Line 410; THRU is wrong. Should be TO.
Line 620; PD is an incorrect variable name.
Line 98; 3X is an incorrect variable name. The step size will not permit the loop to conclude.
Line 25; The comma should be replaced by TO.
Line 15; The word FROM should be replaced by an equal sign.

Lesson 14

```
10 FØR I = 1 TØ 5
   ⋮
60 FØR J = 1 TØ 10
   ⋮
150 FØR K = 1 TØ 3
   ⋮
200 NEXT K
   ⋮
270 NEXT J
   ⋮
300 FØR L = 1 TØ 6
   ⋮
340 NEXT L
   ⋮
375 NEXT I
```

Lesson 15

Line 150; The word MAT is not shown.
Line 180; X1 is an illegal matrix name. X is OK.
Line 200; CONSTANT is illegal; should be CON.
Line 210; The statement is illegal. Write it "MAT X = (1)*Y".
Line 225; Too many matrices shown in the expression. Two is maximum.
Line 250; 3 must be in parentheses.

Lesson 16

```
10  FNY(X) = X ↑ 3 + X ↑ 2
20  FNP(R) = R + 6
30  FND(J) = SIN(J) + CØS(J)
    .  ⎫
    .  ⎬   Statements not shown
    .  ⎭
80  LET  P = SQR(T+W)- FNY(A*B)
85  LET  Q = FNP(R) ↑ 2
90  LET  T = FND(V) / FND(W)
    .  ⎫
    .  ⎬   Statements not shown
    .  ⎭
99999 END
```

Index

A

B

C

Index

C (Continued)

Index

E

F

G

Index

H

I

J

K

L

L (Continued)

M

N

N (Continued)

O

P

R

S

Index

S (Continued)

Index

S (Continued)

T

U

Index

V

W

Z